MODERN CHRISTIAN ART

IS VOLUME

123

OF THE

Twentieth Century Encyclopedia of Catholicism

UNDER SECTION

XII

CATHOLICISM AND THE ARTS

IT IS ALSO THE

133RD

VOLUME IN ORDER OF PUBLICATION

Edited by **HENRI DANIEL-ROPS** *of the Académie Française*

MODERN CHRISTIAN ART

By WINEFRIDE WILSON

HAWTHORN BOOKS · PUBLISHERS · *New York*

First Edition, November, 1965

NIHIL OBSTAT

Joannes M. T. Barton, S.T.D., L.S.S.

   Censor Deputatus

IMPRIMATUR

✠ Georgius L. Craven

   Episcopus Sebastopolis, Vicarius Generalis

Westmonasterii, die XXVII AUGUSTI MCMLXV

CONTENTS

INTRODUCTION

This book is an attempt to sketch in outline one aspect of art in a period which, though far from being a golden age, is not lacking in importance. A philosopher would interpret the term "Christian Art" more widely than my space allows. Maritain says that Church art is "merely an outstanding and peculiar point of applied Christian art"; but although I believe that a landscape by Samuel Palmer can be a Benedicite, and a pierrot by Rouault a Miserere, for the purposes of this book I have confined myself to liturgical art and art devoted to Christian subjects. It has not been possible to do more than indicate general trends, and individual names should be understood as examples, not as a catalogue. Artists who interpret Christian subjects have not been excluded if they are not themselves Christians. The history of art does not bear out the words attributed to Fra Angelico: "To paint the things of Christ you must live Christ." It is somewhat disturbing to find that devout men like Overbeck and Maurice Denis do not paint religious themes in a more convincing way than an unbeliever like Perugino or a homicide like Caravaggio.

One of the reasons is that an artist is always affected to some extent by what his clients and contemporaries expect of him. In an age not necessarily of faith, but of general understanding of Christian beliefs and principles, even an atheist could produce convincing examples of religious art. What the nineteenth century expected was a watered down and sentimental extension of late Baroque. The twentieth century has wiped all the outworn formulas off the slate but does not really know what new demands to make of the artist, who thus works in an atmosphere not necessarily unsympathetic, but often uncomprehending; furthermore, the impersonal patronage of committees and corporations (however enlightened) lacks the inspiration and stimulus provided by individual patrons (however exacting and capricious) like Julius II or Lorenzo the Magnificent.

I have not drawn any distinction between Catholic and Protestant artists, and indeed ecclesiastical patronage has nearly always been ecumenical in outlook. While the Anglican Cathedral of Liverpool was being built to the plans of a Catholic architect, the Catholic Cathedral in the same city was being designed by a member of the Church of England: and statues by Epstein can be found not only in Anglican cathedrals but also on the wall of at least one Catholic convent.

I do not, however, unreservedly subscribe to the opinion that there is no specifically Catholic or Protestant art. Baroque, the only really vigorous movement in Christian art since the Renaissance, has a Counter-Reformation aura about it. Rembrandt is the only artist of the first rank whose work has a recognizably Protestant flavour, but Blake and Stanley Spencer represent unorthodox forms of Protestantism; and the Pre-Raphaelites make a more Protestant (or at least less Catholic) impression than the Lukasbund. Certain differences of treatment have come down to the humblest levels in our time. Cheap Catholic "holy pictures" have inherited the formal set of gestures, the upturned eyes and vaguely classical pink and blue draperies of late Baroque: it is as though their biblical characters cannot forget that they are really Latins out of the Vulgate. Cheap Protestant greetings cards and Sunday School literature, with their preference for oriental costumes and scenery, hark back to Rembrandt: it is as though their biblical characters were conscious of their origins in the Hebrew text.

The book opens in the second half of the eighteenth century because I believe that recent developments in art can only be understood in relation to the break in tradition which occurred at that time. Without the liberating influence of the Romantic Movement the most powerful and expressive aspects of modern art might not have been set free; and without the irresponsibility which is one of the dangers of romanticism, the more anarchic and nihilistic elements would have been inconceivable.

CHAPTER I

THE DOWNFALL
OF REASON

The turbulent spirit of the late eighteenth century did not only express itself in such events as the American Declaration of Independence and the French Revolution. As Goethe's concept of individual man superseded the fading Renaissance vision of the *uomo universale*, a change first noticeable in literature became reflected in all the arts. Both the Classical and Baroque systems were at least temporarily exhausted. The rationalism derived from Cartesian philosophy failed to satisfy the human need for an object of worship and this instinct, denied its normal outlet in religion, transferred itself to the cult of the hero, the sublime, nature, freedom, nationalism and power.

The category of the sublime, in the Romantic sense of the term, was first formulated by Edmund Burke in *A Philosophical Inquiry into the Origin of our Ideas of the Sublime and Beautiful* (1756). Burke suggested that passion might be more important than beauty, which he defined in a rather limited way as associated with such qualities as smoothness, delicacy and grace. Any object of contemplation which was overpowering in its emotional impact was sublime and could give pleasure, even if the feelings which it aroused were painful or terrible. Ugliness was therefore not excluded and ideas such as death, infinity, immensity, obscurity and annihilation were regarded as particularly sublime. Immanuel Kant

in his *Critique of Pure Reason* (1781) attacked the rationalism
of his contemporaries by declaring that reason could only
operate within the limits of experience, and was incompetent
to deal with the transcendent ideas of God, soul and world.
In his *Critique of Judgement* (1790) he supported Burke's
classification of aesthetic responses, but suggested that pleasure in the sublime resulted from the mind's resistance to
tremendous forces: in looking at a "sublime" landscape
(storm clouds, trackless forests, precipitous gorges, etc.) the
spectator was invigorated by a sense of his own superiority
in not being overwhelmed by it.

The Renaissance pre-occupation with outward appearances declined, and emphasis was laid instead on the "inner"
life. From about 1780 the break in tradition becomes
increasingly evident. Romanticism liberated imagination
and stimulated powers of expression at a cost of order, precision and serenity. There was a feeling that man might be
fallen but nature was undefiled, and formal gardening was
replaced by landscape gardening. A consciousness of power
almost amounting to divinity was induced by using trees,
bushes, lawns and hills as units of a vast plan, diverting a
stream here and trapping a lake there. Symmetry was at a
discount and irregularity of any kind was prized, whether it
was the roughness of natural wood, or moss and ivy growing
on a wall. As themes for painting and sculpture rugged
mountains, stormy skies, shipwrecks, battles, wild animals,
primitive tribes, moonlight and ruins were preferred to the
more urbane subjects formerly admired. In architecture the
Middle Ages, long despised as barbarous, were rehabilitated,
though medieval styles were not regarded as worthy of revival for important buildings until the nineteenth century.
They were only used for country churches and as sophisticated jokes in the forms of villas, follies and sham ruins. The
most ambitious example was Horace Walpole's Strawberry
Hill, now a Catholic training college.

One of the earliest manifestations of the Romantic Movement in Germany was Heinrich Wackenroder's book with the cumbersome title of *Herzensergiessungen eines kunstliebenden Klosterbruders* (1797) (A Friar's Meditation on Art). Wackenroder proclaimed that art was a gift from God, a sort of personal revelation. He urged that Christian art, which seemed moribund, should be revived.

The great museums and art galleries of the world are nearly all creations of the nineteenth century or later. The entirely new idea that art was something holy tended to give these public collections the aura of aesthetic temples; and although it was in one way an excellent development that everyone should be enabled to enjoy works which had hitherto been the prerogative of exalted persons, in another way it was regrettable because Christianity became equated with archeology. Where Christ appeared on the same terms as Osiris and Apollo, all religions seemed fused into a pan-religion of art. Altar-pieces and altar plate, reliquaries and cult images were torn from their proper context and lost much of their significance.

To this period belong the first organized exhibitions which led to a new relationship between artist and public. Patronage gradually became less personal, choice of subject was widened, and artistic discipline slackened.

William Blake (1757–1827), born only a year after the publication of Burke's *Inquiry*, was the first known artist since the Middle Ages to be more concerned with inward vision than with accurate representation. He appears on the scene like an unheralded meteor, self-taught and, like most self-taught men, however gifted, with a certain lack of balance and discipline in his thought. He had an abnormally visual imagination: in his case the proverbial "seeing is believing" was reversed. His religious views were so heretical that they almost amounted to an esoteric mythology of his own, but this does not prevent many of his images from being perfectly valid for orthodox believers. He was a lifelong rebel, opposed to any form of authority, whether of Church or State, and he believed the world to be the evil emanation of an evil creator: therefore God the Father was for him a symbol of terror and tyranny, while God the Son, whom he identified with oppressed humanity, was the personification of all beauty and goodness.

Blake scorned the powers of observation so much cultivated by his predecessors, and closed his eyes to outward appearances. He never travelled abroad, and he never troubled to study the human figure from life. His only models were secondhand: engravings after Michelangelo, Raphael and Dürer, details of Gothic revival architecture, and the monuments in Westminster Abbey. This was the pathetic stock-in-trade with which, on scraps of paper sometimes less than three inches square and rarely larger than a quarto sheet, he projected some of the greatest masterpieces of mystic imagination in the whole range of European art. Few other artists could express with a mere linear rhythm so many moods and emotions: perhaps the most beautiful example of what I mean is a curiously typical boneless bending of the neck which gives to his bowed heads every shade of meaning from humility, tenderness, submission and compassion to grief, shame and abasement.

His particular contribution to the history of art is a way of looking at subjects in the sharp focus of the mind's eye before clothing them in the blunter shapes of external vision. His draped figures have a wonderfully fluid quality, and there is a constantly recurring image of a backward-glancing figure turning on one heel which can express regret, yearning, indecision or pity. His heads of Christ often have a serene and unsentimental beauty which is particularly striking in contrast with the tumultuous whirl of figures which often dominates his work.

Among the artists associated with or influenced by Blake,

Flaxman will be referred to in another chapter. Samuel Palmer (1805–81) and Edward Calvert (1799–1883) belonged to a brotherhood known as the "Ancients". Their mystical approach to pastoral subjects owes much to Blake, but Calvert abandoned Christian themes after a visit to Greece had turned his interest to mythology. Palmer may truly be called a religious artist, for his entire early output was a hymn of praise, full of Christian symbolism. He illustrated a number of biblical subjects but undertook no major religious works, and later in his career he lost the burning-glass intensity of his vision. By a curious coincidence his source of inspiration, like Calvert's, seems to have deserted him after a visit abroad—in his case, to Italy: but his influence can be traced in the work of most subsequent English painters of Romantic landscape, including Sutherland.

Goya (Francisco de Goya y Lucientes, 1746–1828) was almost Blake's contemporary. He was a much greater painter and a major figure in the history of art, but religious subjects were not a prominent feature of his output and from this angle his influence was negligible. The romantic element can be detected in his work from about 1790, when a more sombre, tragic and satirical mood replaced his earlier Rococo style. He has often been called the last of the Old Masters and the first modern painter, and it is true that although he is still concerned with outward appearances his sense of actuality looked forward to the Impressionists rather than back to the Renaissance. His most important ecclesiastical commission was for the frescoes in San Antonio de la Florida, Madrid. They are not only technically interesting (being executed apparently with a sponge) but are examples of religious subjects interpreted in popular contemporary terms.

Outside South Germany, Austria and Switzerland, where there was a splendid florescence of Rococo architecture, the later eighteenth century was not a period of active church building in Europe. In most countries the legacies of more fervent times were adequate for current needs. This was the case with the Established Church in England, where Catholics were still an underprivileged minority, worshipping for the most part in the chapels of embassies or private houses. The rise of Methodism, however, led to an increase in the number of nonconformist meeting houses, which usually followed the style of Wren. The typical interior was provided with a gallery, and the most prominent feature was a pulpit half-way along one side with a communion table in front of it.

Before the revivalist movements of the nineteenth century crossed the Atlantic, there were two main traditions of church building in America. In the north-eastern states, English colonists were instrumental in establishing pleasantly sober and dignified styles reminiscent of Wren. In the west and in Central and South America, a more exuberant style of Baroque inspiration was introduced by Franciscan and Jesuit missionaries. American painting and sculpture in this period were, as they had been since the seventeenth century, heavily indebted to Europe; but the academic principles advocated by Reynolds proved more enduring than in the country of their origin. The French Neo-Classical painter David declared that the best painters of the English school were all Americans (Benjamin West, John Singleton Copley and Ralph Earl all settled for a time in London), but his opinion was no doubt coloured by his republican sympathies and his preference for works in the grand manner. Benjamin West (1738–1820) was a founder member of the Royal Academy and succeeded Reynolds as its president. As a young man he spent three years in Rome, Florence, Venice and Bologna. American painters were such a novelty in Italy that Cardinal Albani, who was blind, was surprised to learn that he was not a Red Indian. Benjamin West painted twenty-eight subjects from the Old and New Testaments, all of heroic proportions, which must have been one of the most prodigious undertakings since the Renaissance. They were much imitated, in France as well as in the English-speaking countries.

Sometimes these versions must have been very free for William Dunlap (1766–1839), in his autobiography, describes how in 1822 he painted a vast picture based merely on a printed description of West's "Christ Rejected". It was customary at that time for large religious paintings to be transported round the United States in travelling shows. Most of them have disappeared, but we can be sure that they were usually pedestrian examples of the grand manner. They were displayed in churches where the parson might preach a sermon on the subject, or in halls where the artist or his agent might deliver a lecture. Rembrandt Peale (1778–1860) earned 8,000 dollars in a year with his enormous "Moral Allegory", now in Detroit museum. Other American painters of religious subjects were Washington Allston (1779–1843), William Jewett (1812–73), Robert W. Weir (1803–89) and Daniel Huntingdon (1816–1906). In England at the same period, Benjamin Robert Haydon (1786–1846) and John ("Mad") Martin (1789–1854) were producing huge, spectacular biblical scenes which were the nineteenth-century equivalent of twentieth-century Hollywood epics. I was told by an eyewitness that, as recently as 1909, vast canvasses in this tradition were still being displayed in Aberdeen in halls such as the Y.M.C.A. at an admission fee of six cents.

Although there was no really indigenous school in America, there were two traditions which seem to have more national character than the imported art of the academies. One of these was the primitive style which grew up among amateurs and artisans, carvers of figureheads, and other anonymous craftsmen, mostly in the north-eastern states; the other was the style which developed in the mission territories, a kind of exotic Baroque. In every country where Baroque art has become acclimatized, it has been interpreted with much charm and success by peasant craftsmen, for its dramatic and ecstatic qualities appeal instinctively to simple people. Long after it ceased to be a living force in more sophisticated societies, it continued to be favoured as a style for religious art at a popular level, and the blending of Spanish idioms with elements of native Indian cultures produced some very lively and attractive works. It is only in recent years, however, that their merit has been recognized, and the woodcarvings of humble craftsmen have become more sought after than the pretentious Neo-Classical white marble of their professional contemporaries.

CHAPTER II

NOSTALGIC BROTHERHOODS

We have seen in the previous chapter that Wackenroder regarded art as a divine revelation, demanding a devout approach from both artist and spectator. Friedrich Schlegel (1772–1829) was more specific. He not only insisted with Wackenroder that Christian art must be revived; he also provided the nostrum which, according to him, consisted of a return to the methods of the old German masters and of Italian painters before Raphael. Schlegel became a Catholic and a number of artists followed his example.

In 1808, a group of young painters in Vienna decided that the Vienna Academy was corrupt and had outlived its usefulness. So many groups have seceded from academies in more recent times that we may not realize what a momentous step this first secession was on the part of the Lukasbund, or company of St Luke, which was the name adopted by the group. In 1810, under the leadership of Friedrich Overbeck (1789–1869) and Franz Pforr (1788–1812), they left for Rome where they adopted a community life in the deserted monastery of S. Isidoro. The other pioneer members were Hottinger, Sutter, Vogel and Wintergerst, soon to be joined by Ferdinand von Olivier (1785–1841), Peter von Cornelius (1783–1867), Julius Schnorr von Carolsfeld (1794–1872) and others. Several of the Lukasbrüder, including Overbeck, became Catholics and were nicknamed the "Nazarenes";

derisive epithets such as "religious patriotic" were applied to the work of the group.

The aim of the Lukasbund was to combat the materialistic spirit of the age with an art that was in the direct Christian tradition. Their standards of sincerity and craftsmanship were high, and they recognized that much of the decorative quality of medieval painting lay in its abstract patterns. They are still dismissed as "stiff", "lifeless", "anaemic" and "aesthetic failures" by critics who do not seem to recognize that their use of two-dimensional design and areas of flat local colour anticipated Puvis de Chavannes and Gauguin by many years. It is true however, that they lacked some vital spark, and as they developed their work lost much of its simplicity. They were strongly influenced by Dürer as well as by Italian primitives, and this led some of them to include the smallest details, outlining every blade of grass with very sharp pens and very fine brushes. Fresco painting was regarded as the noblest form of art, and they tried to recapture the spirit of a medieval workshop when they collaborated on frescoes in the Casa Bartholdy (now in Berlin) and the Casino Massimo.

Cornelius was the least romantic and the most monumental in style. He later became the head of the academy in Munich, where with the help of his pupils he decorated the Ludwigskirche. Overbeck's inspiration was purely Italian, but Pforr was more deeply indebted to late medieval German painting. A shortened version of Schnorr's *Die Bibel in Bildern* was published in England in 1860 under the title of "Schnorr's Bible Pictures".

The Lukasbrüder are more important for their influence on Ingres, other German Romantics and the Pre-Raphaelites than for their actual output; but their idealism and their quiet conviction constitute a refreshing oasis in a period of overstatement. Their medieval nostalgia rather than their other qualities had an indirect effect on church architecture, furnishing and decoration in Germany, and they were the forerunners of the Düsseldorf school. These included Edward von Steinle, who was a prolific painter of rather mawkish church murals in a style which unfortunately spread to America.

A Scottish painter, William Dyce (1806–64), was the link between the Nazarenes and the Pre-Raphaelites. He had studied in Rome and his precise, cleanly painted Madonna, commissioned by the Prince Consort and executed in 1828, was the means of introducing the Lukasbund style to England. The Pre-Raphaelite Brotherhood was founded in 1848 by William Holman Hunt (1827–1910), John Everett Millais (1829–96) and Dante Gabriel Rossetti (1828–82), and was joined by Rossetti's literary brother William Michael, a minor painter called James Collinson, Thomas Woolner the sculptor, and F. G. Stephens who began as a painter and later became an art critic. The cryptic initials P. R. B. first appeared on Rossetti's painting "The Girlhood of Mary Virgin", exhibited in 1849.

The members of the Brotherhood were dissatisfied with the trite academism of their contemporaries which could be classified into two types: sentimental genre painting and ambitious history-painting in the outworn grand manner. Because Reynolds had based his rules on the art of the Italian Renaissance, they made Raphael the scapegoat for all the shortcomings of nineteenth-century painting; in fact, they knew nothing of Raphael and had never seen early Italian art except in engravings. The name Pre-Raphaelite had already been applied more aptly to the Nazarenes; but although the Germans were better art historians, the English were better painters. The chief quality which was lacking in the Nazarenes was passion, and the Pre-Raphaelites had more than their share, allied with a peculiarly English kind of high moral purpose. Their work was less specifically religious than that of the Nazarenes, but Christian subjects were frequently chosen, such as Hunt's "Light of the World", Millais's "Christ in the House of his Parents" and Rossetti's "Annunciation". Their idea of truth was not, as Blake's had been, faithfulness to some inward vision; it was rather a reverence for actual appearances which must be copied from nature as literally as possible. Of the three founders, Rossetti had the most poetic imagination and the least technical skill: Millais was less intellectual but far more accomplished: Hunt was the most deeply sincere, and the only one who remained committed to the original principles of the Brotherhood throughout his career.

The Pre-Raphaelites were among the most literary of painters and subject-matter was of great importance to them. One of the evils that they wished to avoid was a generalized "ideal form", so every inch of the canvas had to be worked up to the detailed brilliance of jewellery. They achieved an effect of vivid clarity by their method of launching pure, bright, transparent colours into a wet white ground. Compared with their innocent colouring, the palettes of other painters tended to look muddy and adulterated. Rossetti was less devoted to naturalism than the others (or perhaps he lacked the skill required for such a polished performance) and his painting, usually in a highly individual water-colour technique inspired by illuminated manuscripts, was almost two-dimensional in effect. Millais's rather unimaginative pursuit of visual truth is illustrated by his insistence on using a real carpenter as his model for St Joseph in "Christ in the House of his Parents", a picture which elicited an ignorant and ill-natured attack from Dickens. Hunt was perhaps the most Protestant painter since Rembrandt.

Connected with the Brotherhood, but not actually members, were Ford Madox Brown (1821–93), Arthur Hughes (1832–1915), and the short-lived Walter Deverell (1827–54). Of these, Brown was the most considerable painter. He had a broader style and had studied on the Continent where, like

Dyce, he had actually met the Nazarenes. The work of Arthur Hughes, full of purples and greens, has a gentle, melancholy, tender charm that barely avoids sentimentality. Other figures hovered on the fringe of the movement, and there was a secondary wave in which William Morris (1834–96) and Edward Burne-Jones (1833–1898) were associated with Rossetti. This was a rather decadent, languid, mannered phase which fostered an insipid kind of aestheticism; but the Arts and Crafts Movement sponsored by Morris encouraged good workmanship and was one of the trends in the direction of *art nouveau*.

Later in the century Dom Desiderius Lenz (1832–1928), assisted by two other monks (Lukas Steiner and Gabriel Wüger), started a school of art at the Abbey of Beuron. Their first products were influenced by the Nazarenes, but later Dom Desiderius developed a stiff, hieratic style of his own which was vaguely Egyptian in inspiration. His theories about religious art never found popular acceptance but they gained some adherents in "advanced" circles on the Continent, especially in other Benedictine communities. The most notable decorative schemes of the Beuron School—paintings, altar-pieces, fonts and other church furnishings—were carried out in the abbeys of Beuron itself, Emmaus, Monte Cassino and Prague, between 1870 and 1913. They influenced Father Benedict Williamson, who produced a number of neo-Egyptian decorative schemes in the early years of the present century, notably in the London churches of St Ignatius, Stamford Hill; St Boniface, Tooting; and the Lithuanian Church in Hackney Road.

CHAPTER III

THE AGE OF REVIVALS

The nineteenth century was an archeologically minded period and its architectural history is one of revivals.

The Greek and Gothic revivals flourished concurrently in England in the earlier part of the century. The neo-Classicism of the eighteenth century, influenced by the discoveries of Pompeii and Herculaneum, had been Roman in emphasis; even its major prophets, such as Winckelmann, were almost entirely ignorant of Greek originals. The publication of Stuart and Revett's *Antiquities of Athens* in 1762 fired other travellers to visit the country, and the arrival in England of the Elgin marbles (1801) aroused enthusiasm for the "purer" architecture of Greece. The so-called Grecian style was popular in England until about 1840, and its application to English church architecture will be considered in the next chapter. It was seen to great advantage in Scotland where Alexander Thomson chose it for his three fine Presbyterian churches in Glasgow—St Vincent Street, Caledonia Road and Queens Park: and where Edinburgh's New Town (largely the work of Craig and Playfair) rivalled Berlin, Copenhagen, Munich and St Petersburg as a "romantic classical" city. The style spread to the British possessions overseas and was taken to the United States by Benjamin Henry Latrobe (1764–1820). In addition to working on the Capitol, he was responsible for the excellent Catholic cathedral in Baltimore, which is not unlike Soufflot's Panthéon (1790) in plan.

In France, J. F. T. Chalgrin's Saint-Philippe-du-Roule was

the prototype for a number of barrel-vaulted, basilica-type churches, respectable but uninspired. It was French influence rather than any autochthonous school that succeeded colonial Baroque in South America; and a French architect built St Isaac's cathedral in St Petersburg, technically interesting at that date (about 1842) for its iron-framed dome.

In Germany, the outstanding architects were Karl Friedrich Schinkel (1781–1841) whose most celebrated church—the Werdersche Kirche in Berlin—was an imitation of English Gothic and therefore not really typical of his monumental style: and Leopold von Klenze (1784–1864), architect to the King of Bavaria, for whom he built the somewhat Byzantine Royal Chapel in Munich. He also designed the Catholic Cathedral (Aghios Dionysus) in Athens. Klenze's rival, Friedrich von Gärtner (1792–1847), was the architect of the almost Romanesque Ludwigskirche in Munich. The round arched style, not uncommon in Germanic and Scandinavian countries at that time, was known as the *Rundbogenstil*. There was an attempt, more or less confined to the years between about 1835–40, to popularize an eclectic kind of Romanesque in England, but it did not gain much ground. Later in the century, however, Henry Hobson Richardson (1838–86) revived it with some success in the United States.

By far the most widespread and persistent of the revivals was the Gothic. In the same way that the Greek Revival was one aspect of the Neo-Classic movement, the Gothic revival was one aspect of the Romantic movement. While the Greek revival was welcomed by scholars, the Gothic revival had a much more general appeal: there was at least some truth in Walpole's assertion that "one must have taste to be sensible of the beauties of Grecian architecture; one only wants passion to feel Gothic". Although the cult of medieval ruins and tombs showed itself in the work of the "graveyard" poets and the Gothic novelists before it affected architecture, it would be true to say that Gothic architecture had never completely died, even when it had been superseded by Renaissance styles. Throughout the seventeenth century isolated churches were being built which were survivals rather than revivals. Among these were Low Ham in Somerset (1634), and the private chapel at Staunton Harold, Leicestershire (1653–65), built by the Anglican Sir Robert Shirley as an anti-Cromwellian gesture. Laud's church of St John, Leeds (1634) was Gothic with some classic ornaments. The first conscious imitations were probably restricted to towers, such as those of St Mary's, Warwick (1694), and some of Wren's city churches. In the second half of the eighteenth century, country churches were sometimes rebuilt in a kind of "Rococo Gothick"; they were not Gothic in construction but were tricked out with neo-medieval elements such as pointed windows and battlemented parapets. The textbook example of this type is at Shobdon, Herefordshire (1753).

The Gothic revival properly so-called may be divided into two phases. The first grew out of the "picturesque" style just described, in which antiquarian "correctness" was not the aim. St Peter's Chapel at Winchester, designed by John Carter for Bishop Milner in 1792, is usually regarded as the prototype, and the chapel of St Mary's Seminary, Baltimore (1807) is the first example of any significance in North America, followed by Notre Dame, Montreal (1824). The second phase, in which more importance was attached to structure, grew out of Pugin's two great principles of design: that "there should be no features about a building which are not necessary for convenience, construction or propriety", and "all ornament should consist of enrichment of the essential construction of the building".

The Gothic style became so firmly entrenched in the popular imagination that even today many people feel that no other kind of building "looks like a church". The Gospel according to Pugin—that the later Middle Ages produced the only valid form of Christian architecture—is still with us. It seems curious that the period of the Black Death and the Great Schism should be regarded as a golden age. Why, one might ask, should it be considered more truly Christian than the apostolic age? Why should the noble achievements of Byzantine and Romanesque art be more limited in their appeal? Why should not Christians in the twentieth century feel stimulated by the idea of dedicating new materials and new techniques for the glory of God? The explanation is not a simple one, for both intellectual and emotional responses are involved. Educated enthusiasts have seen in Gothic architecture the first style evolved exclusively for Christian worship. It was a tremendous engineering discovery developed and perfected in the service of the Church. Its principles were not applied to secular buildings until a century or more later, whereas the earlier types of churches such as basilicas, mausolea and martyria had all been adapted from profane use. The pointed arch, it is true, had probably been imported from infidel sources, but it was not an essential feature of the construction as the ribbed vault was; yet it is the pointed arch, more than anything else, which stamps a building as Gothic in the eyes of humble worshippers. How is this preference to be explained? It is probably threefold. In the first place, Gothic is the most familiar style of ecclesiastical architecture in North-West Europe, whether it dates from the Middle Ages or the nineteenth century, and people tend to like what they know. Secondly, to the simple mind the most complicated work seems the most admirable, and the solid masses of Romanesque buildings, the classical orders of post-Fire of London churches, and the austere lines of modern architecture do not suggest the same manual dexterity as flying buttresses, elaborate tracery, fan vaulting and fretted screens. Thirdly, a building can convey religious feeling by creating awe or by creating ecstasy; and most people would rather be uplifted by the vertical sweep and transmitted light of a Gothic nave than forced to their knees by the transcendent atmosphere of a Byzantine interior. In Southern Europe ecstasy is well served by Baroque and Rococo, which in the north tend to look frivolous as a result of their frequent adaptation to rather tawdry ends; and in Latin countries none of the nineteenth-century revivals made much impact.

The Gothic revival was altogether less productive on the continent of Europe than it was in the United States and the British Empire. It was not regarded as a universal style. There was no French equivalent of the great flood of English churches, which will be considered in the next chapter, partly because there was not the same need for them; but there was a profound theoretical interest in Gothic construction. French neo-Gothic churches seem to have been planned without the intensity of purpose that went into English churches of the same period, and they nearly always look hard and cold. It is not surprising that English architects won competitions abroad, George Gilbert Scott for the Nikolaikirche at Hamburg, and Henry Clutton and William Burges for Lille Cathedral (with George Edmund Street taking the second prize). The Chapel Royal of Saint-Louis at Dreux was remodelled from a classical rotunda to a rather Rococo Gothic style, with stained glass by Ingres and Delacroix; but the only French church of this period with much character and distinction is Saint-Pierre-de-Montrouge in Paris which is not Gothic at all but a sort of Syrian Romanesque. Its architect, J. A. E. Vaudremer, may have influenced the American H. H. Richardson, who was a student in Paris at the time.

In France, Germany and Holland there was great activity in the restoration of medieval buildings. Eugène Viollet-le-Duc (1814–79) might have been better employed in designing new churches than in restoring ancient cathedrals, for his Saint-Denys-de-l'Estrée (at Saint-Denis), vaulted in stone throughout, is better than many of its contemporaries. His *Dictionnaire raisonné de l'architecture française du onzième au seizième siècle*, in ten volumes, of which the first appeared in 1854, became the Bible of continental church furnishers and exerted a world-wide influence comparable with Ruskin's. He restored many national monuments including the Sainte-Chapelle, the Madeleine at Vézélay, Saint-Denis and Notre-Dame de Paris, often with more enthusiasm than discretion.

In Germany the major restoration was of Cologne cathedral, and among the new churches, de Chateauneuf's Petrikirche in Hamburg was one of the more successful. In Vienna, Schmidt's Fünfhaus parish church is more original than von Ferstel's Votivkirche, and in Holland Petrus Josephus Hubertus Cuijpers' Maria Magdelenakerk (Amsterdam) is perhaps the most impressive of the many freely adapted Gothic churches built by him. Cuijpers (1827–1921) was a follower of Viollet-le-Duc who "stood at the crossroads between historicism and the modern movement in the Netherlands" (J. J. Vriend).

CHAPTER IV

PREACHING BOXES AND TRUE PRINCIPLES

The mid-twentieth century has coined for its own problems phrases which would have been equally applicable in the early nineteenth century; for the Industrial Revolution too had its "brain drain" and its "population explosion", when the more enterprising inhabitants of the English countryside flocked to seek their fortunes in the towns.

To meet the needs of these new urban communities, the Church Building Act of 1818 voted a million pounds towards the cost of building churches in industrial areas. Half the available accomodation was to be devoted to "free seats for the poor". One would like to believe that concern for the souls of mill-hands and factory workers was behind this decision; but the principal motives were probably alarm at the spread of Dissent and fear that the labouring classes would become infected with revolutionary ideas. The more voices that could be raised against such dangerous tendencies the better; and it is significant that all these new places of worship (variously known as Commissioners', Waterloo or "Million" churches) were built on the principle that hearing the preacher was more important than seeing the altar.

The Million Pound Fund was administered by the Lords Commissioners of the Treasury who drew up stringent requirements and scrutinized all the plans submitted. Although the utmost economy was enjoined and little scope

left for the designer's imagination, most of the leading
architects of the period co-operated in the scheme, including
John Nash (1752–1835), Sir John Soane (1753–1837), Sir
Charles Barry (1795–1860), Sir Robert Smirke (1781–1867)
and Charles Cockerell (1788–1863). Nearly three hundred
churches were built between 1819 and 1830 and, with the aid
of subsequent grants, about six hundred churches were
built altogether as a result of this campaign.

On the whole the Commissioners' churches were respec-
tably built in a way which accorded well enough with routine
domestic Georgian architecture. Recommended styles were
Neo-Greek and Neo-Gothic but, because of the rigid conditions laid down, style in most cases had to be a matter of
superficial ornament, not of construction. Stripped of their
classical porticoes or medieval trappings, they have four
marks by which we may know them: a rectangular plan, the
altar in a shallow chancel at the east end, galleries on the
other three sides, and double rows of windows on the north
and south walls. A paved area surrounded the building, and
there was usually an organ in the west gallery, a prominent
pulpit at one side of the altar and a reading desk at the other;
but Victorian restorers who sneered at the Commissioners'
churches for being cheap and nasty did their best to make
them unrecognizable, adding mosaic and stained glass to
create a "Lombardic" or "Byzantine" effect in the Grecian
type, and breaking up the interior space of the Gothic type
with chapels and a deeper chancel. Sir Arthur Blomfield
(1829–99), the son of a bishop of London, had a talent almost
amounting to a perverse genius for this sort of transforma-
tion scene. Even after his treatment there is a further means
of identification for which I am indebted to Mr John
Betjeman: Commissioners' churches are generally to be
found in that part of a town where the streets have Hano-
verian names such as Adelaide, Brunswick, Hanover, Nelson
or Regent. Some of the recommendations of the Lords

Commissioners make fascinating reading today: "If vaulted underneath, the crypt is to be made available for the reception of coals or the parish fire-engine" is particularly evocative.

Among the Grecian type St James's, Bermondsey (1827) is one of the more successful; and its architect, James Savage, was also responsible for St Luke's, Chelsea (1820), which was exceptional for its period in having a groined stone vault and flying buttresses instead of a mere flavour of Gothic. The Perpendicular of St Peter's, Brighton (1823), by Sir Charles Barry, is also rather more than skin deep and is therefore ahead of its time. At this point mention must be made of the most ambitious of the Greek revival churches, although its cost was not met by the Commissioners. The parish church of St Pancras, London (1819–22), which cost over £70,000—a vast sum in those days—was paid for by public subscription and a levy on the rates. The work of the Inwoods, father and son, it has been much admired but combines too many different elements for perfection, including a caryatid porch inspired by the Erechtheion and a steeple, adapted from the Temple of the Winds, surmounted by an imitation of the monument of Lysicrates. Probably the best of the Neo-Romanesque churches is Christ Church, Streatham (1841–2), by J. Wild.

After the Catholic Emancipation Act of 1829 it became possible to build Catholic churches again. At first these tended to be Italianate, in a Renaissance-cum-Romanesque style. As a rule they were basilican in plan and may have been influenced by the King of Bavaria's great new basilica at Munich, or by the rebuilding of St Paul-outside-the-walls in Rome. Their ornament was usually Baroque in feeling, sometimes charming but more often crude or flimsy. Examples were St Raphael, Kingston-on-Thames (1846), overlooking the river like some handsome Tuscan villa, and St Mary's, Grantham (1832).

The motive power behind the second phase of the Gothic

revival was Augustus Welby Pugin (1812–52). If Chesterton was right when he said that the nineteenth century saw the Middle Ages by moonlight, no one was more moonstruck than Pugin; but the same moon had already cast its spell on his father, whose influence on the Gothic revival is often overlooked. Pugin *père* was a French emigré who had found employment as a draughtsman in the office of John Nash, to whom his artistic ability and wide knowledge of Gothic architecture and ornament proved invaluable. He published a number of books on the subject which his son helped to illustrate. He also conducted a residential atelier for architectural students at his own house in Islington and it was there that his son received his first training. Pugin *fils* was not only brilliant but immensely industrious. Noble-hearted and wrong-headed, he had all the qualities which go to make a fanatic; and in his short life he accomplished, so his doctor claimed, the work of a hundred years. Catholic Emancipation was still something of a novelty when, in spite of a Calvinistic mother and "without being acquainted with a single priest, by God's mercy" he found his way into the Church. He lost no time in making himself thoroughly unpopular with his new co-religionists. Shocked by the post-Tridentine atmosphere of Catholicism as he found it, he began to campaign for a return to pre-Reformation usages. The Fathers of the Oratory incurred his most opprobrious censures: they were "worse than the Socialists". Books and articles poured from his tireless pen, his most important publications being *Contrasts between the Architecture of the 15th and 19th Centuries* (1836); *The True Principles of Pointed or Christian Architecture* (1841); *An Apology for the Revival of Christian Architecture in England* (1843); *A Glossary of Ecclesiastical Ornament* (1844) and *A Treatise on Chancel Screens and Rood Lofts* (1851). Gothic to him was not merely one possible style among several; it was one of the articles of his Creed.

Pugin's ideals seem peculiarly unacceptable in the era of the Second Vatican Council, when all the emphasis is on full participation of the laity: for he was obsessed by the concept of the mysterious, privileged, and sacrificial aspect of the priestly office, which he thought should be surrounded by secrecy. He thought it monstrous that an altar should be overlooked, and insisted on a screened-in chancel with a rood-loft. "Well may we exclaim," he said, "when passing beneath the image of our Redeemer, and through the separating screen of mystic import into this holy place, *O quam terribile est locus iste*." The principle that the whole congregation should be able to see the action (which had its advocates even then) was only applicable to theatres in Pugin's opinion. On the other hand, he thought it proper for penitents to confess their sins in full view (and presumably earshot) of their fellows, for confessional boxes were, he assured them, unheard of in the ages of faith. He might never have had an opportunity to build and decorate a church exactly as he wished had not an unbelievably generous and compliant patron rallied to his support. St Giles's, Cheadle, was built at the expense of Lord Shrewsbury, for whom Pugin designed Scarisbrooke Hall in Lancashire. Other important works included St George's Cathedral, Southwark (since destroyed by enemy action and restored), St Chad's Cathedral, Birmingham, and many collegiate and conventual buildings in England, Ireland and Jersey. He built two houses for his own use, of which the second—the Grange, Ramsgate—had a church attached and is now part of a Benedictine abbey.

The *True Principles* was translated into French and published at Bruges in 1850. Thereafter, Bruges became one of the chief centres for supplying church furniture in accordance with Pugin's views.

It might be thought that such a man would have been entirely humourless. On the contrary, he often displayed a pretty wit and a nice line in satire. His illustrations of "The extravagent style of Modern Gothic Furniture and Decoration" and "An Emporium of Fashion" remind one of Osbert Lancaster; and he observes tartly: "All the modern plans of suspending folds of stuff over poles, as if for the purpose of sale or of being dried, are quite contrary to the use or intention of curtains." In *Contrasts*, while the drawings of fifteenth-century architecture are peopled with idealized Chaucerian pilgrims and priests in dignified vestments, the nineteenth-century scenes are full of wretched beggars and vulgar representatives of the bourgeoisie, against a background of caricatured "pagan" buildings. In describing a prosperous merchant's house he says: "On one side of the house machicolated parapets, embrasures, bastions, and all the show of strong defence, and round the corner of the building a conservatory leading to the principal rooms, through which a whole company of horsemen might penetrate at one smash into the heart of the mansion!—for who would hammer against nailed portals when he could kick his way through the greenhouse?"

Pugin's influence was enormous and out of all proportion to the quality of his own architectural output, in which he could never quite express the beauty of which he dreamed. He fired other young architects with an enthusiasm only inferior to his own, and young Gilbert Scott must have spoken for many when he said: "Pugin's articles excited me almost to fury, and I suddenly found myself like a person awakened from a long, feverish dream." When Pugin died, worn out and mad, he left behind a host of disciples who could be relied on to perpetuate his teaching. All over England, from Hackney to Sheffield, from Burnley to Greenwich, Catholic churches were rising in accordance with "the true principles".

That Pugin's perfervid zeal should have swept his fellow Catholics along in its wake is not, perhaps, so remarkable;

but that he should have bemused the Established Church into accepting buildings and fittings adapted for a form of worship repudiated by its members is an extraordinary achievement. It is true that Dean Close (famous for his thunderings against tobacco, horse-racing and theatres), preached a Guy Fawkes day sermon on "the restoration of churches is the restoration of popery"; but not long afterwards he too succumbed and built himself a cruciform "Norman" chapel with an apsidal chancel. Pugin was helped by the fact that the time was ripe for a medieval movement within the Church of England. Before any of his books were published, the Tractarians at Oxford and the Camden Society at Cambridge were campaigning for the restoration of some forms of pre-Reformation ceremonial. Newman himself was a medieval enthusiast to the extent that, in later years, he used to make a memento in his Mass of Sir Walter Scott, whose writings he believed to have contributed to the Catholic revival in England.

The Camden Society was formed in 1839 by two undergraduates, John Mason Neale and Benjamin Webb, who subsequently became clergymen. At first the society was largely composed of graduates and undergraduates at Cambridge, but membership spread to a cross section of the Church of England. Their outlook was not primarily aesthetic, being concerned with architecture and church furnishing as a frame for ritual; but as the ritual which they had in mind was for a high Anglican type of worship, they approved of the churches which were being designed by Pugin. Although they acknowledged him as the master, they held very strong views about employing practising Anglicans on the building of Anglican churches. A journal called the *Ecclesiologist* was founded in 1841, and in 1845 the more progressive members broke away and formed themselves into the Ecclesiological Society. The movement spread abroad and New York had its own *Ecclesiologist*.

The instructions and judgements of this society make the Sacred Congregation of Rites appear almost latitudinarian; and journals which today publish lists of new churches, with stars to recommend the best buildings, cannot equal the forthrightness of the *Ecclesiologist's* classifications: P for Praised, M for Mediocre and C for Condemned. Architects too were divided into sheep and goats under headings of "Approved" and "Condemned". Several American churches were approved, including Holy Cross, Troy, New York; St Mark's, Philadelphia; and the Advent Church, Boston. Mr Peter Anson tells us that rectory ladies devoured this publication as though it were "a sort of early Victorian ecclesiastical equivalent of *Vogue*".

Thomas Rickman's classification of English Gothic into Early English, Decorated and Perpendicular (proposed in 1817 and still in use) was translated by the Ecclesiologists into Early, Middle and Late Pointed. Pugin preferred the term "Pointed" as being more accurate than the scornful "Gothic". To the Ecclesiologists, Middle Pointed represented perfection, Early Pointed being considered crude and Late Pointed decadent. High on the *Ecclesiologist's* "approved" list was Richard Cromwell Carpenter (1812–55), architect of St Nicholas, Kemerton, Glos. (described by the late Mr Goodhart-Rendel as "The Tractarian Paradise"); St Mary Magdalene's, Munster Square, London; St Paul's, Brighton; Lancing College Chapel; and St John's Chapel, Hurstpierpoint. Carpenter was Pugin's exact contemporary and friend, and was considered by the *Ecclesiologist* to be "superior even to Pugin, safer and more equable". He was, in fact, less advanced than Pugin, from whom he often borrowed ideas and adapted them to Anglican use, but he was not lacking in sensibility.

If judged by productivity and worldly success, Sir George Gilbert Scott (1811–78) would rank as the outstanding practitioner of his day; but his was not an original mind and he was the organizer of an efficient factory rather than a great architect. He employed an army of assistants, and plans for a prodigious number of cathedrals, churches and public buildings issued from his office, including the Albert Memorial, Glasgow University, St Pancras Station, St Mary's Cathedral, Edinburgh and St Mary Abbots, Kensington. It is doubtful if his personal share was very considerable in his later years, but he can sometimes be recognized by certain characteristics such as a preference for open spaces, groups of three equal lancets surmounted by a round window, and plate tracery. He founded a dynasty of architects still active in the fourth generation, and many young men trained in his office achieved the highest distinction in their profession.

Much more interesting, both as an architect and as a personality, was William Butterfield (1814–1900). Pugin, in spite of his eccentricities, remains a sympathetic character; William Butterfield creates a singularly unendearing impression. The contrast between the man and his works amounts almost to paradox. Dour, ascetic, puritanical, celibate, uncompromising, he moved only in High Anglican circles and scarcely acknowledged the existence of such contemporaries as Pugin, Scott and Street. His buildings were challenging in their originality, vigour and vulgarity. His name is particularly associated with "permanent polychromy", which would never have proved acceptable to his clients if Ruskin had not taught people to look at Italian architecture with its zebra stripes and banded marbles. Butterfield did not like mural paintings because they were not part of the structure. His colour was provided by assorted granites, marbles, serpentines, alabasters, glazed bricks and encaustic tiles. As Mr John Summerson has said: "There was no *colour scheme*: merely a childish belief that natural materials arranged in geometrical patterns are sure to be right. . . . All Butterfield's churches are to a greater or less degree ugly. And in almost all there is power and originality transcending the ugliness."

It was not possible to be comfortable in buildings which he designed. He disapproved of heating and seating, so he made both as penitential as he could by devising inconvenient charcoal braziers and benches which made sitting a much worse hardship than kneeling. He did not believe in chancel screens and side altars, and he wasted no time on pretty perspective drawings for his clients. Scaffolding and ladders had to be dusted before he would set foot on them. One of his more successful churches is at Baldersby St James in Yorkshire. There, the polychromy is less strident than at (for example) All Saints, Margaret Street, London, which is remarkable for his ingenious manipulation of a cramped and overshadowed site. Much of the spirit went out of Butterfield's later work, although he continued to be active almost until the end of the century. Scott, Butterfield and Carpenter designed churches all over the British Empire.

Constructional polychromy became one of the characteristics of High Victorian building. It was exploited with some success by George Edmund Street (1824–81), one of Scott's "young men" who became a leading figure. His work has a massive quality and the Law Courts in London was one of his most important but not one of his happiest undertakings. He was himself a Tractarian who sang in the choir at Wantage. He designed churches for a number of Anglican communities abroad, and for American communities in Paris and Rome, the latter being one of the best examples. He favoured a single altar visible from all parts of the church. Although he too had an enormous practice, he carried out every detail of the work himself, and somehow found time to write useful books on Italian and Spanish architecture. Morris, Philip Webb, Norman Shaw and J. D. Sedding were his pupils.

In the latter half of the nineteenth century such a forest of spires sprang up in the English-speaking world that it is not possible to keep pace with developments. One must,

however, mention such names as John Loughborough
Pearson (1817–97), another Tractarian, who always prayed
for guidance and received Communion before embarking on
a design. He paid a great deal of attention to the exterior
silhouette of his buildings, which included Brisbane Cathedral, probably the best of the Australian cathedrals, and
Truro Cathedral. Other successful works were St John's,
Red Lion Square (unfortunately destroyed by bombs in the
Second World War) and St Augustine's, Kilburn, both in
London. In his later churches he moved away from the idea
of a single central space, and made provision for side altars
and sometimes for a tabernacle.

William Burges (1827–81) threw himself into the Gothic
revival with such enthusiasm that he tried to live a medieval
life in his Kensington house. His most important ecclesiastical building is St Finbarr's Cathedral, Cork, Ireland, where
the details are rather archeologically influenced by French
twelfth-century work, but the wing which he designed for
Trinity College, Hartford, Connecticut, is the best example
of Victorian Gothic collegiate architecture in the world.

George Frederick Bodley (1827–1907), another of Scott's
pupils, designed the cathedrals at Washington, San
Francisco, and Hobart, Tasmania, in collaboration with
James Vaughan.

John Dando Sedding (1838–91) younger brother of
another architect (Edmund) built a number of churches
including Holy Trinity, Sloane Street, and the Holy Redeemer, Clerkenwell, both in London, and was associated
with the Arts and Crafts Movement.

At least two remarkable churches were built in England by
less celebrated architects. St Peter's Catholic church at Leamington, Warwickshire, was the work of Henry Clutton
(1819–93). Pugin's campaign for chancel screens had not
evoked a really enduring response, and in the last third of
the nineteenth century most Catholic churches reverted to a

more or less basilican plan. In St Peter's, Leamington, the nave continues into an apse, and the barrel vault ends in a half-dome at the east end. Clutton, as we have already noted, had won the competition for Lille Cathedral in collaboration with William Burges, and his familiarity with early French work has obviously influenced this design. St Peter's is contemporary with Viollet-le-Duc's St Denys-de-l'Estrée but is superior in every respect; and it is interesting to remember that Viollet-le-Duc enjoyed an international reputation while Clutton did not, even in England, rank as a leading architect. The adjoining presbytery, which was also built to his plans, is in many ways an improvement on the famous Red House which Philip Webb designed for Morris.

St Bartholomew's, Brighton, has all the grandeur and boldness characteristic of High Victorian Gothic, but it was built by a local Sussex architect—Edmund Scott—who seems to have left no other notable memorials. Here again, the atmosphere of sacred mystery has been dispensed with in favour of a dramatic use of space. St Bartholomew's is like a great dark ark with its interior void uninterrupted by aisles or chancel, and it creates something of the transcendent and monumental impression of a Romanesque basilica.

Gothic continued to be the favoured style in the Antipodes, where Pugin's pupil Wardell built the Catholic cathedrals in Melbourne (begun 1849) and Sydney (begun 1868, the year that the Anglican cathedral was finished). Adelaide Cathedral (1870) was based on designs by Pugin. After 1870, local talent was increasingly used, although St Paul's Cathedral, Melbourne, is one of Butterfield's late works.

Canada struck a different note by building Montreal Cathedral (1860) as a half-size replica of St Peter's, Rome.

The Founder and first President of the American Institute of Architects was the English-born Richard Upjohn (1802–78). When he rebuilt the old Colonial style Trinity Church in

New York, the Gothic style which he adopted (not unlike Pugin's St Marie's, Derby) was an innovation. St Thomas's Church, New York, was on similar lines, but although Upjohn's fame chiefly rests on his contribution to the Gothic revival, he also favoured Italianate and a sort of *Rundbogen-stil*, while some of his country churches were timber constructions. He was a strict Ecclesiologist and only liked using Gothic for Episcopalians.

In the United States, we have seen that H. H. Richardson initiated a Romanesque revival, but his work was not merely archaeological: he had a genuinely original approach. He had studied and worked in Paris (being Louisiana-born he was bilingual) but he was an admirer of Burges, and English high Victorian treatment was often imposed on French forms. He produced polychromatic or at least polytextural effects by employing local stones in imaginative combinations. For Trinity Church, Boston, he used pink Melford granite lavishly trimmed with Longmeadow brownstone. The Romanesque flavour of this building is somewhat mixed, with hints of Auvergne and of the old cathedral in Salamanca. It also contains Burne-Jones glass which is inferior to the small windows by the American artist John La Farge, who also decorated the walls and ceiling. Richardson did not entirely disregard Gothic influence, which he interpreted in a very personal way at the Grace Episcopal Church, Melford, Mass. (1867–8).

When one looks back on the post-Pugin period of the Gothic revival, one is saddened by the tremendous amount of vigour, talent and good sound craftsmanship which was spent on fanning the embers of a style long after its flame had flickered out. With few exceptions, the church architects of the nineteenth century hankered after a dream world that never was, while bridge builders and rail-road engineers seized the initiative that should have been theirs.

CHAPTER V

RELIGIOUS PAINTING AND EUROPEAN MOVEMENTS

If the history of architecture in the nineteenth century is one of revivals, that of painting is a record of movements which continue into the twentieth century, becoming increasingly numerous, climactic and revolutionary. Some of them were ephemeral while others were so momentous that they changed the whole direction of pictorial art; but nearly all produced some examples of religious painting. The only notable excep- *Note* tion was Impressionism which was, as Mr Eric Newton has said, "the last assault in the long cycle that had begun with Giotto, on the world of appearances". As such, in spite of the beauty and importance of its works, it is the most super- ficial of all forms of painting. In the same way that the camera can catch the spontaneous gesture or the fleeting ex- pression, but lacks the insight of a good portrait painter, so the snapshot vision of Impressionism is not the medium for expressing eternal truths. This does not mean that its influence cannot be traced in subsequent religious painting. Colour and light could never look quite the same after the Impressionists had revealed them in a new way.

Blake was an isolated phenomenon for whom time did not exist, while the Lukasbund and the Pre-Raphaelites tried to put the clock back; but after Neo-Classicism the trend was usually forward, so it has seemed convenient to treat the main stream of nineteenth- and twentieth-century painting

as a continuous journey into the future. We have seen that
"Romantic Classical" architecture was a fairly widespread
style while Neo-Gothic was strongest in English-speaking
countries. For painting, the centre of gravity moved to
France, where it remained until the rise of the New York
school in the mid-twentieth century.

During the first half of the nineteenth century there was
some rivalry between the Neo-Classicists, whose high-
priests were David and Ingres, and the romantics, whose
most distinguished representatives were Delacroix and
Géricault. Gabriel-Francois Doyen (1726–1806) had a foot
in both camps, for although he seems to have influenced
David, his *Sainte-Geneviève interceding for the Victims of the
Plague* (St Roch, Paris) and his decorations in the Invalides
and the Ecole Militaire reveal him as a forerunner of the
Romantics. He was celebrated for his altar-pieces. Jacques
Louis David (1748–1825), whose objects of worship were
antiquity and the Republic, has no place in a history of
Christian art except as a great teacher, whose many famous
pupils included Ingres and Gros. It is true that he painted a
*Saint-Roch begging the Virgin to intercede for the Plague-
stricken* (in the chapel of the Fever Hospital, Marseilles), a
commission passed on to him by Vien; but its chief interest
is in its studies of the sick and the dying, which anticipate
Delacroix's *Massacres*. Apart from this David's only
"saints" were the martyrs of the revolution, Saint-Fargeau
and Marat; and the only processions which he designed were
in honour of the Goddess of Reason. With Ingres (1780–
1867) the case was different. Although he found his principal
employment in portraits, he shared Gainsborough's lack of
enthusiasm for "face-painting". He received a number of
important commissions for religious subjects, but it must be
admitted that his influence in this respect was rather unfortunate. Some of the most pedestrian painters of religious
pictures based their style on his and, lacking his superb

draughtsmanship and knowledge of the form under the dra-
pery, produced lifeless academic compositions of which
versions can be bought to this day in the shadow of Saint-
Sulpice. Ingres has two characteristics in common with
Botticelli, although the general effect of his painting is as far
as it could be from that of the Florentine master. The first is
his wonderful snaky line. The second is the fact that his
Virgins and Venuses are indistinguishable; but whereas
Botticelli's Venuses are all virgins, the women painted by
Ingres, whether Virgins, Venuses, houris or rich men's wives,
are all wax dolls. The Ingres face infiltrated into every
stratum of nineteenth-century art. The engravers could cut
nothing else, and every popular print and fashion plate of
the period seems to have its placid, bun-faced, doe-eyed,
button-mouthed beauty. "Drawing is the probity of art",
said Ingres, and indeed few draughtsmen have surpassed
him; but his handling of paint suggests that he regarded
colour merely as something to be added to a drawing. His
reverence for Raphael and Poussin made him strive so hard
for serenity and balance that he smoothed all the life out of
his figures. His "Vow of Louis XIII" also betrays the cool,
detached influence of Philippe de Champaigne, who was at
his best as a portrait painter and at his worst when he painted
pink-and-blue angels. Ingres was not attracted by this subject, which was commissioned for Montauban Cathedral,
and wanted to paint an Assumption instead; but the picture
was acclaimed by the critics when it was exhibited in the
Salon in 1824. It was probably this success which made him
so indignant when his "Martyrdom of Saint-Symphorien"
(painted for the cathedral at Autun, where it still hangs) was
sharply criticized. Among his other religious works are
"Christ handing the keys to St Peter", commissioned for the
Roman church of Trinità dei Monte but now in the Louvre;
and "Jesus among the Doctors", commissioned by Louis-
Philippe for the Chapel Royal at Bizy, but now in the Ingres

Museum at Montauban. It was his practice to make as many as two hundred studies before embarking on a major work, and all his draped figures began as nudes. Some of these sketches, which can be seen at Montauban, have far more movement and expression than the finished paintings.

Eugène Delacroix (1798–1863) was the noblest Romantic of them all. His relationship to Théodore Géricault (1791–1824) was somewhat like that of Titian to Giorgione. In each case a short-lived genius whose reputation rests on a few canvases influenced a younger man who lived on to become a great master with an enormous output. Géricault himself did not leave any memorable religious works, but without his inspiration Delacroix might have been a very different painter. Delacroix had all the fire that Ingres lacked, and a formidable intellect to keep his passion and intensity under control. He was a theorist as well as a painter of tremendous industry and talent, and he had a very French respect for reason and tradition, which lent a wild civility to the ordered disorder of his compositions. He had no respect for Ingres, however, of whom he said: "His art is the complete expression of an incomplete intelligence." He is widely recognized as the liberator of colour and the forerunner of the Impressionists, and his typically Romantic subjects are well-known—battles and massacres, wild animals, heroic and exotic scenes—but his very considerable religious œuvre is less familiar. The first commission which he ever received was for a "Madonna of the Harvest" (in the church at Orcemont). He was twenty-one when he painted it, and showed little sign of his future powers. It betrays his indebtness to Raphael, and no doubt he thought himself adequately paid with fifteen francs; thirty years later, he was to receive 26,826 francs for decorating the Chapel of the Angels in Saint-Sulpice. In these large scale murals (other examples are in the Louvre, the Chamber of Deputies and the Town Hall at Rouen) he is not seen at his best, for he employed a number of assistants. A very interesting early work is "Our Lady of the Sacred Heart" (in the cathedral at Ajaccio). Géricault was originally asked to execute this commission but it did not appeal to him, and he asked Delacroix to undertake it in his place. Delacroix too seems to have been taxed by the unusual and difficult subject, for a number of studies preserved in the Louvre reveal his indecision. The final version shows our Lady looking rather like a robust personification of the Republic, clutching a cross instead of the French flag. He returned again and again to subjects of his choice, such as Crucifixions, Depositions and Pietàs, which *Note* allowed him to show his skill in painting stormy skies, darkness over the earth, and human grief and desolation.

There is a very fine Crucifixion in the Walters Art Gallery, *Note* Baltimore, and another in the Municipal Museum at Vannes. In these, and in the Entombment in the Museum of Fine Arts, Boston (of which there is a replica at Zurich) the influence of Titian and Rubens is very marked. Another favourite subject was St Sebastian, the most celebrated example being the one admired by Baudelaire in the church at Nantua. The Brooklyn Museum owns a "Disciples at Emmaus", and the most important of several versions of the "Agony in the Garden" is in the church of St Paul and St Louis in Paris. The latter had a mixed reception from the critics when it first appeared. Delacroix painted the "Storm on the Lake of Gennesareth" at least ten times, sometimes with a rowing boat (as in the Art Museum, Portland) and sometimes with a sailing boat (as in the Walters Art Gallery, Baltimore). The subject had all the elements that a Romantic artist could desire. But there is one picture painted by Delacroix which has none of the turbulence and drama that we expect. "The Education of the Virgin", now in a private collection in Paris, was painted in George Sand's garden at Nohant, and the models were her godchild and her maid. The group has a gentle and tranquil air and our Lady wears a charmingly rustic mob cap. Some years later, Delacroix painted another small canvas from the same sketches, and this is now in the National Museum at Tokyo.

The early history of Jean-François Millet (1814–75) reads like a piece of conventional hagiography. All the best legends begin with the hero or heroine guarding sheep. Millet was no exception and, like Giotto, he whiled away the time by drawing. He was fortunate in his parents, who recognized the merit of his work, and in the village curé, who supervised his education. At the age of twelve he was reading the Georgics in Latin, and his favourite books were said to be the Confessions of St Augustine and the Letters of St Jerome. Among modern writers he preferred Fénelon and Pascal, but the influences which remained with him through-out his life were the Bible and Virgil. When he first began to pursue the career of an artist in Paris he painted clever pastiches of mildly erotic eighteenth-century works, until an incident occurred which made him turn his back on these frivolities. According to Alfred Sensier, his first biographer, he stopped to glance in a shop window which was displaying some of his work and happened to overhear one passer-by say to another: "Who painted that picture?" The reply was: "Why, Millet, of course; he paints nothing but nudes." This conversation seems to have caused him much mortification, and he immediately made a resolve never again to paint erotic subjects. With very few lapses (as he would have regarded them) or happy exceptions (as they would appear to admirers of his nudes) he kept this resolution for the rest of his life. One is at liberty to think that this denial of one facet of his art may have put a brake on his creativity. If he had joyfully accepted his sensuality as a good Christian like Rubens did, his colour might have been less dingy, his handling less laboured, and his forms less lumpy; for after all, one can be true to nature and still see fresh colours in the countryside and graceful figures in the harvest field. In the completeness of his "conversion" Millet seemed to be trying to repudiate the false view of the country conveyed by courtly pastorals, and to show instead only the heaviness of toil and the coarseness of peasant life. He always disclaimed any moral or social message in his work, and indeed the resignation with which his peasants seem to be accepting their lot supports his denial of any revolutionary or even radical tendencies. "I want", he said, "the people to look as if they were dedicated to their station—that it would be impossible for them ever to think of being anything but what they are."

Millet's "Angelus" (originally exhibited in the Exposition Universelle of 1867 as "l'Angélus du Soir") is said to have been reproduced more often than any other work, including the Sistine Madonna and the Mona Lisa. It has hung in the parlours of thousands of dwellings whose owners must have regarded its subject as idolatrous or superstitious. It is not by any standards a pretty picture. The colour is muddy, the forms are clumsy, and it lacks even that meticulous treatment of detail which usually appeals to popular taste. Its secret is the way in which Millet was able to combine a classic concentration on a few immutable forms with a romantic vision surviving from his "Fragonard" days. Anyone can see at a glance what it is about, for the images are all pre-digested. The afterglow in the sky tells us that it is evening, the church steeple on the horizon tells us that the bell is ringing, the fork thrust in the soil tells us that the day's work is done, clasped hands, bowed heads and doffed cap all unite in telling us that the people are praying; and they are not just any people but Man and Woman, the human race. They will have a long walk home, because there is no human habitation in sight. Their cottage is sure to be in a group clustered round the distant church.

This picture did Millet's reputation among later critics immeasurable harm. That is a pity, for he was a fine draughtsman and an artist of integrity, capable of creating noble,

massive compositions. Although he usually restricted himself to a group of two figures on a single plane he could,
when he wished, manage much more complex arrangements
such as that seen in "Ruth and Booz" (Museum of Fine Art,
Boston). America is very rich in Millet's paintings and
drawings, partly owing to the enthusiasm of William Morris
Hunt, a young American artist who knew Millet in Paris and
introduced his work to the United States when he returned
there in 1855.

The entry of Japan into trade relations with the West had
a far-reaching effect on European art. Cheap coloured
woodcuts, despised by Japanese connoisseurs, were often
used as wrappings in consignments of merchandise, and
artists of Manet's circle were the first to discover their aesthetic merits. Here was a magic world in two dimensions,
where no shadows fell and where sudden areas of velvety
black drew attention to strangely restful empty spaces, about
which the artist had found nothing that he wanted to say.
The flat washes of colour in Japanese woodcuts was to prove
a more lasting attraction than the Impressionist's flickering
brushstrokes.

John La Farge (1835–1910), the most distinguished
American painter of religious subjects in the second half of
the nineteenth century, may be mentioned here because
Japan was one of the important sources of his inspiration.
He was of French parentage and was something of a poly-
math. Although he showed artistic talent as a boy and was
given lessons by his maternal grandfather (a miniaturist) and
by an English water-colour painter, he began his career as a
lawyer. In 1856 he went to Paris where he decided to study
art seriously; but he did not intend at this stage to become a
practising artist, as he explained when he presented himself
as a pupil to Thomas Couture (1815–79). In the Paris of
Baudelaire, Gautier and Victor Hugo, Couture was highly
esteemed, but he is now chiefly remembered as the master of

Manet. La Farge only remained in his studio for about a fortnight, finding it more to his taste to study the Old Masters in the Louvre and other great European collections. He visited Munich, Dresden, Belgium, Denmark and England. In later years he travelled in Japan and the South Seas. He read Ruskin and was impressed by the Pre-Raphaelites. When he returned to New York he continued to read law for a time, but he eventually came to devote himself to painting, writing and lecturing on art. He was invited by H. H. Richardson to paint murals for Trinity Church, Boston, a project in which he was assisted by Francis David Millet (1846–1912). He also painted panels for the Church of the Incarnation in New York, but his masterpiece of religious painting was probably the mural of the Ascension inspired by a Japanese landscape, in the Church of the Ascension, New York. He did much to revive the craft of stained glass in America. He developed a type of glass known as "opaline" and designed windows rather in the style of Burne-Jones and Morris, but richer in colour.

Jean Tissot, though better known for his popular *genre* paintings, spent ten years in Palestine for the purpose of giving authenticity to his illustrations for the New Testament.

Pierre Cécile Puvis de Chavannes (1824–98) was another pupil of Couture. His most notable work is the series of mural paintings of the life of Sainte-Geneviève in the Panthéon, but he also decorated many other official buildings including the Hotel de Ville in Paris and the library at Boston, Mass. Almost every important painter of the post-Impressionist period expressed admiration for his work and acknowledged his influence. Although he painted in oils on canvas cemented to the wall, he achieved something of the effect of fresco. His style was almost primitive, with simple linear rhythms and pale flat colours. He had the "respect for the wall" which one finds in Romanesque murals, never attempting any tricks of illusionist perspective.

Puvis de Chavannes did not call himself a Symbolist but he was associated with Symbolism, which, like the Gothic revival, was a literary movement before it affected the visual arts. It originated in the poetry of Mallarmé, Rimbaud and their circle. When applied to painting it describes an attempt to express subjective ideas, moods and emotions in terms of form and colour. In practice, this resulted in a rejection of naturalistic representation and of the broken colour developed by the Impressionists, and a return to flat simple forms and local colour. It is a rather confusing movement because some of its adherents referred to their method of painting as Synthetism or Cloisonnism.

Odilon Redon (1840–1916), although regarded as a Symbolist, was really too independent and introspective to become completely integrated with the group, but the creations of his fantastic imagination were certainly typical of the Symbolist attitude; he may also have influenced the Surrealists. In the earlier part of his career he concentrated almost entirely on lithography, producing limited series of prints which included an Apocalypse and three sets of "Temptations of St Antony" based on Flaubert; but after 1890 he began to produce more paintings, acknowledging Delacroix as a primary influence and achieving an iridescent quality in his colouring. As a religious artist he will be remembered for one of the few tolerable representations of the Sacred Heart, though it must be admitted that he rather evaded the difficulties by leaving the subject deliberately vague and dreamlike.

Another aspect of the movement can be seen in the work of Paul Gauguin (1848–1903) and his Pont Aven associates, Émile Bernard (who claimed to have invented Synthetism) and Paul Sérusier. They exhibited their work as Synthetists, and their paintings, which were intended to be syntheses of the ideas which inspired them, featured brilliant flat colours kept apart by black lines in the same way that the enamel is separated by metal plates in cloisonné work; during this period in Brittany Gauguin painted several religious subjects including "Jacob wrestling with the Angel" (Glasgow Art Gallery), and the "Christ Jaune" (Rosenberg Collection) which sums up very well the characteristics of the Pont Aven group.

With Georges Rouault (1871–1958) we come to the most powerful religious artist of modern times. He belonged to no group (although he exhibited with Matisse and the Fauves in 1905) but he could be classified as an Expressionist. Expressionism is not in essence a twentieth-century innovation. It is found, for instance, in the work of Grünewald and other Old German masters (Grünewald's dates belong to the Renaissance but his spirit was medieval); but it did not become a concerted movement until the early years of the twentieth century, when it was represented by (among others) Van Gogh, Edvard Munch, Kokoschka and Chaim Soutine, and by two groups—"Die Brücke" and "Der Blaue Reiter". It seems to be a North European phenomenon and is characterized by an attempt to project strong emotion by such means as violent colour and distorted form.

Rouault's art was not, like that of many German Expressionists, hysterical. All the intense feeling that went into it was disciplined by an armature of leaden lines, not necessarily separating the colours as in Cloisonnism, but rather containing them as in stained glass. Rouault was, in fact, apprenticed at the age of fourteen to a maker of stained glass, and it is a matter for regret that he always refused to practise this craft (although some windows were made from his designs). One suspects that, quite unconsciously perhaps, the man who belonged to a family of skilled craftsmen felt that the "fine arts" carried more prestige. Although one thinks of him instinctively as a colourist, he was criticized as a young man for his excessively sombre palette. Moreau at one stage was afraid that his favourite pupil would become obsessed with Rembrandt, but although Rouault learned much from Rembrandt technically, his colour gradually caught fire and glowed with a richness that is not put to shame by the glass of Chartres and Bourges. The ruggedness of his forms and his rejection of non-essentials would have made his art acceptable in Romanesque times. Uncompromisingly modern though he may appear to some observers, he was essentially a traditional artist. Subject-matter was immensely important to him. He was a moralist who regarded the vices and foibles of humanity not with the bitterness of Goya or the amused tolerance of Hogarth or the indignation of Daumier (although Daumier must have been a strong influence) but with a profound pity and regret. When he painted prostitutes, as he often did, particularly between 1903 and 1907, he stripped them of every hint of glamour and emphasized only the degradation, ugliness and squalor. The idea of one man sitting in judgement on another was so repugnant to him that he made judges scapegoats, and showed them as symbols of worldly corruption. He leaned heavily on symbols and liked to paint clowns as types of the artist or prophet—lonely men, laughed at and misunderstood by the crowd. Many of these were self portraits which reveal the solitude of a devout man surrounded by an atmosphere of unbelief.

Like Blake, Rouault could express almost any emotion in the mere gesture of a bent neck. Like Picasso, he could turn from brutality to tenderness, and could convey an impression of youth or innocence with exquisite delicacy. He was not an outstanding draughtsman, but in his etchings which are as important a part of his œuvre as his paintings, he evolved techniques which could produce images of great power and beauty. He used to draw the design in India ink and transfer it to copperplate by a variety of means—files, rollers, scrapers, needles, sandpaper and brushloads of acid. He was never satisfied with the results and often made a dozen or more states of one etching. His canvases, too, were constantly reworked, and in his old age he destroyed more than three hundred pictures.

"My only ambition", Rouault once said, "is to be able *NB* one day to paint Christ so movingly that those who see Him will be converted." Perhaps this was why he nearly always chose to paint the "Sacred Head ill-used". His intensely subjective vision of Christ is a restricted one in which, as in all his work, pity for suffering humanity seems to be the dominant feeling, associated with a sense of human responsibility. He fails, or does not try, to show us Christ in Majesty or Christ in Judgement—it is always Christ the Victim, Christ mocked, Christ weighed down by our sins.

There is no question that Rouault towers head and shoulders above any other religious painter of his time, but it is legitimate to ask how he compares with the great figures of the past. He did not see the whole of creation with new eyes as Giotto did. He lacks the spacious calm of Piero della Francesca, and he cannot match the virtuosity of the High Renaissance masters. He has none of Rubens's huge joyful inventiveness and he did not, like Rembrandt, find heaven and earth on his back doorstep. But it seems to me that he achieves a higher degree of spirituality than any of these, and can be compared rather with those artists, often anonymous, who have left us transcendent images in the form of Byzantine mosaics, Romanesque frescoes and Russian icons.

Matisse was a fellow student with Rouault under Moreau. It was only at the end of his life that he conceived the idea of creating a religious work of art, but when the inspiration came to him he acted upon it in a dedicated spirit and a wholesale manner. As the project was not strictly concerned with painting, it will be described in subsequent chapters.

Expressionism has been on the whole the most fruitful movement in the religious painting of the twentieth century.

It is exemplified at the present day by the work of Graham Sutherland (b. 1903) who enjoys the greatest prestige of any living British painter. He is a Romantic artist in the direct line of descent from Samuel Palmer, and was regarded primarily as a painter of landscape until that enlightened patron Dean (then Canon) Hussey asked him to paint a Crucifixion for St Matthew's, Northampton. Out of this commission grew a great many studies and related subjects such as the "Thorn Heads". Sutherland's religious work to date is as limited in range as Rouault's. His vision is tragic and sombre, and it is always the Crucifixion and its attendant events that he chooses to paint, though he designed, with some misgivings, the great tapestry of Christ in Majesty for Coventry Cathedral (referred to in a later chapter). His Crucifixions are in the tradition of Grünewald, not calmly accepting but tortured and writhing. It seems to me that his religious work is to some extent inhibited by a conscious effort to avoid the Christian iconography of the past, and also by a difficulty in evolving what he calls "a valid equivalent for tenderness . . . because the Church in the main (and I am not speaking of any particular Church) in associating itself for so long in modern times with an art of banal and empty sentimentality, would with rare exceptions be unlikely to tolerate new and vital conceptions in this field". Although Sutherland is a Catholic, his first important religious commissions (for Northampton, Coventry and Chichester) were for the Church of England; but he has more recently painted a Crucifixion for the Catholic Church at East Acton, London.

Another living artist whose religious work may be included in this category is the French painter Bernard Buffet (b. 1924). A number of critics affect to disregard him, perhaps because he is a successful and immensely prolific painter of still life, landscape and other popular subjects; and also, perhaps, because he has achieved a certain modishness in spite of having refused to swim with the fashionable stream of abstraction. When Buffet bought the Château l'Arc near Aix-en-Provence, the private chapel was neglected and ruinous. He determined to restore and redecorate it, and in 1961 it was reopened with the celebration of Midnight Mass. One of the congregation remarked that the priest at the altar and the Crucifixion figure behind seemed so united in the sacrifice that it was difficult to believe that the painting had not been there from time immemorial. This statement seems to point to an authentic Christian art, for the painting is not immediately attractive to the eye. It is angular and spiky and the emphasis is on human agony, not on triumph over sin and death. Buffet himself says that he is not conscious of Gothic influence, but this is so marked that one can isolate actual elements derived from medieval paintings (for example, the drapery of some of his figures is very close to that of hovering angels by the Meister des Hausbuchs); but there are also strong affinities, notably in the heavy black outlines, with Catalonian Romanesque wall paintings. The method which Buffet used was similar to that of Puvis de Chavannes, though the results are very different. The paintings are in oil on canvas attached to the wall, and the subjects include the Nativity, the Baptism of Christ, the Last Supper, the Veil of Veronica and a Pietà, as well as the Crucifixion already mentioned.

Of the same generation as Buffet is Francis Souza (b. 1924) an artist from Goa in whom the conflicting elements of popular Portuguese Baroque, Indian bazaar painting and Hindu erotic sculpture have interacted to produce a dangerously explosive mixture. Neither are these the only influences that can be traced in his brand of Expressionism, which is almost unique in not being a product of northern Europe. It is obvious that he has also been impressed by Byzantine and Spanish Romanesque art, and by the painting of El Greco. There is a wilful immaturity about his work that reminds one of Picasso, from whom he seems to have borrowed certain disruptions of the human form. Although Souza is a Catholic, he has so far been neglected by ecclesiastical patronage which, though disappointing, is not altogether surprising: for the emotional impact of his work is often achieved by violent distortions which some observers might find irreverent. His crucified Christ is the image of the Suffering Servant carried to extreme limits: "No stateliness here, no majesty, no beauty, as we gaze upon him, to win our hearts." Souza sometimes uses primitive forms of imagery such as many eyes shedding tears to suggest grief, streams of blood spurting like jets from a hose, enormously enlarged hands and feet to emphasize the Sacred Wounds; but for all his vulgarity (and no art was ever more remote from good taste) there is great power, rich colour and a splendid hieratic quality in his best work which makes one hope that it may yet be used in the service of the Church.

It is now necessary to go back to the end of the nineteenth century, to a small group of French painters convened by Paul Sérusier (whom we have already met at Pont Aven with Gauguin). He called this group the Nabis or Prophets, after the Hebrew word Nabiim, "the divinely inspired". The most important members were Maurice Denis (1870–1943), the theoretician of the movement, Bonnard, Vuillard and the sculptor Maillol. Bonnard and Vuillard were the most painterly of them and came to be placed in an even smaller group of their own known as Intimistes, because they usually painted interiors. As a group, the Nabis attached great importance to subject-matter, partly because they were influenced by the Symbolist writers. Like the Symbolists, they aimed at giving their ideas aesthetic form. They reacted strongly against Impressionism and painted in pure, flat colours. Their programme is summed up by the sub-title of Maurice Denis's book *Théories*: "From Symbolism and

Gauguin toward a new Classic Order". It was in this book that Denis made the pronouncement which is regarded as one of the basic principles of twentieth-century art: "Remember that a picture, before being a battle-horse, a nude woman or some kind of anecdote, is essentially a surface covered with colours assembled in a certain order."

Maurice Denis was a devout Catholic, and with Georges Desvallières he founded a School of Sacred Art planned not on the lines of an academy but on those of a studio-workshop for apprentices. Unfortunately, although his theories of religious art were excellent, his own work (infinitely better though it was than most of the religious "art" then being produced) did not quite live up to his ideals, and Desvallière's was worse. Denis was a talented painter who produced fine easel pictures such as the *Hommage à Cézanne* in the Louvre, but to present-day eyes, his religious work often looks mawkish. Conservative though it now appears, it was thought revolutionary in his own time, and was much criticized and misunderstood. After completing the decorations in the church of Vésinet (Seine-et-Oise) in 1899, he found little outlet for his religious work except in his own private oratory in the priory at Saint-Germain-en-Laye, for which he painted murals and Stations of the Cross, and designed windows. It was fifteen years before he was given another important commission—the vast apse of the church of St Paul in Geneva. Here his earlier, more intimate style expanded to an almost Baroque vision. In addition to his large mural schemes in the church of Saint-Esprit, Avenue Daumesnil, Paris, Saint-Louis at Vincennes, the Franciscan Chapel at Rouen, the War Memorial Chapel at Gagny and the Palais de Chaillot, he designed windows for the church of Notre-Dame du Raincy, Paris, and illustrated many books including the Imitation of Christ, the Fioretti of St Francis, the Life of St Dominic, and Georges Goyau's *Histoire Religieuse de la France*. He himself wrote a monumental

Histoire de l'Art Religieux. Although his work lacks the flame that burns in Rouault's it has a quality of candour and innocence that is very remarkable in an artist who, far from being simple or primitive, was an intellectual surrounded by a sophisticated society.

Unlike the Nabis, the Fauves were a group without very coherent aims. Their work was hung together in one room at the Salon d'Automne in Paris in 1905 and was character-ized by flat patterns, distorted forms and violent colouring. The name *Fauves*, meaning wild beasts, was applied in derision by a critic. Rouault, Matisse and Braque were among the many celebrated artists who exhibited with this group, which disintegrated after about two years.

Paul Cézanne (1839–1906) was probably the most im-portant figure in the whole period covered by this book, although he made no specific contributions to religious art. Considered purely as a painter he may not have been so great as Goya or Turner, so radiant as Renoir or so versatile as Picasso; but with him painting came to the end of the road which it had been following since Giotto pointed the way. If this road had seemed less clearly marked to Blake it was only because he walked along it with eyes shut, seeing only his own visionary world; but Cézanne had his eyes wide open and it seemed to him to end in a swamp, through which he must find some solid ground to walk on.

Cézanne's typical style is so classical that it is difficult to reconcile it with the Romantic work of his youth, when he inclined towards sensational and often erotic subjects painted in a technique inspired by Delacroix. With maturity he acquired more control, and became dissatisfied with the lack of formal qualities in Impressionism. While accepting its optical discoveries which had revolutionized the artist's palette, he deplored the transitory nature of its vision. He wanted to retain its chromatic scale, but at the same time to convey the essential structure under the accidental appearance. By his much-quoted remark that he "wanted to do Poussin again, from nature", he meant that he wanted to combine the Impressionist's revelations about light and colour with the order and balance found in Poussin. His researches were long and laborious, and many of his pictures were abandoned because he was not achieving the end he sought; but eventually he evolved a method of painting which, as it were, made Impressionism vertebrate. By treating colour and tone as one thing, the colour *became* the modelling. By varying the direction of his brushstrokes he built up a solid structure which, compared with the work of Monet, Pissarro and Sisley, seems to represent the earth's crust and core while they could only describe its atmospheric envelope. His exploration of the interrelationship of forms led him to dispense with academic rules of perspective: for instance, if he were painting a still-life of objects on a table, he did not scruple to tip the plane of the table surface forward so that more of its contents could be seen. This and his search for a geometrical framework in nature, led logically and almost inevitably to Cubism, which carried his ideas a stage further.

Picasso (b. 1881) and Braque (1882–1963), influenced also by the conceptual nature of negro sculpture (which had impressed European artists even more forcibly than Japanese prints), formulated together a more intellectual basis for pictorial art. This entailed expressing the whole idea of an object rather than a single view of it; in other words, in one picture they attempted to move all round the forms, combining and sometimes superimposing several aspects of each. The first stage of fully developed Cubism (1909–12) is described as Analytical because forms were being broken down and examined from different angles. Colour was reduced almost to monochrome and in one phase (known as Hermetic Cubism) subjects became very difficult to read. The final development (1912–14), which we call Synthetic, was less pure but more decorative, as it was marked by a return to the use of colour, an increased legibility, and a more positive attitude towards the subject. Humpty Dumpty was being put together again.

Cubism did not at that time produce any religious art, though Braque (as will be recounted later) designed some stained glass windows for churches, and a great deal of modern glass is abstract with a Cubist flavour. We shall also see that abstract art in general, which was the natural outcome of Cubism, has been adopted extensively for religious use. It is a matter of regret that Picasso has not to date placed his great gifts at the service of the Church, although he has painted at least one Crucifixion (1930) which is still in his own collection. He began to make drawings for this work in 1927, and in 1932 he produced a further series of studies based on Grünewald's Isenheim altar-piece, many of which contain elements that reappear in *Guernica* (1937).

The only important religious painter who has been strongly influenced by Cubism is Roy de Maistre (b. 1894). In the vanguard of Australian artists who have in recent years achieved a considerable reputation in Europe, he seems much more a product of the École de Paris than of the contemporary Australian School. He is more cerebral, complex and urbane than most of them, with a sense of style which is the exact opposite of a rather raw vigour which one tends to expect from his fellow-countrymen. It is true that he is of French descent and has spent the greater part of his mature life in Europe, but even before he left Australia his paintings were more formal and schematic than was customary in one of his New South Wales background and training. He is essentially a connoisseur's painter and has never achieved widespread popularity or even due recognition. There are two possible reasons for this. He is indifferent to the saleability of his works and continues to paint as he feels impelled, regardless of the number of canvases that pile up in his studio (which tends to look like a permanent retrospective exhibition); he is a man of deep reserve and although his pictures are often very pleasing to the eye, his vision is so personal that it is sometimes almost esoteric—but not in the heterodox sense of Blake. Although I have included him at this point for convenience, he cannot really be classified as a Cubist. He is open to many influences (he once told me that he was "like blotting paper") so that he is sometimes almost Surrealist and at others almost abstract; and in his very extensive religious œuvre, which involves strong personal convictions, there are often traces of Expressionism. This is particularly noticeable in paintings of the passion of our Lord. As a rule, his work achieves its greatest impact when it is most simplified. The finest example is probably the Pietà in the Tate Gallery, with its few strong colours and its stark black lines ripping ruthless diagonals across the canvas. The Thirteenth Station in the set of Stations of the Cross which he made for Westminster Cathedral is similar. He has painted a great many versions of the Crucifixion which might be described as variations on a theme, including those in the Leicester City Art Gallery and the Art Gallery of New South Wales. It is his custom to start work by making a naturalistic representation of his subject, and then to discard non-essentials by degrees, at the same time adding conceptual elements. For instance, in painting a portrait he may eliminate some descriptive passage but add something that he knows or remembers about the sitter. In this way, nearly all his pictures undergo a series of states like an etching, often becoming increasingly abstract. He is not an outstanding draughtsman but he has a fine colour sense and he has, like Cézanne, found a way of expressing structure in terms of colour.

Albert Gleizes (1881–1953), one of the original Cubist circle who surrounded Picasso and Braque, devoted himself to religious painting after going to America in 1917. He combined traditional Catholic iconography with his own flat, geometrical, decorative technique, and also wrote on the subject. For ten years, from 1921 to 1931, Evie Hone (1894–1955) and Mainie Jellett worked for a period each year in his studio. They were his first pupils, and his style and methods were more congenial to them than those of André Lhôte with whom they had previously worked. It is sometimes forgotten that Evie Hone was thirty-eight years old and an established painter before she turned to stained glass, and she continued throughout her life to work in oils, gouache, and graphic media. It is interesting to note that she was descended from a long line of distinguished painters, one of whom (Nathaniel Hone II) had been an associate of the Barbizon group.

Fernand Léger (1881–1955) was also influenced by Cubism but he developed a style of his own that was more curvilinear and based on forms used in machinery, such as cog-wheels and cylinders. There was a strongly decorative element in his work with its bold black outlines, primary colours and greys. He has designed splendid mosaics and windows for churches, which will be referred to in the appropriate chapter.

It is difficult to relate Alexandre Cingria (1879–1945) to any specific movement, but as he belongs to this period he is included here. Born at Geneva and Swiss by nationality, his father was an Italian from Ragusa and his mother was Polish. He also had French blood, and this convergence of cultures in his ancestry, combined with a receptive imagination and a theoretical knowledge of the art of many periods and nations, probably contributed to the eclecticism of his own style. This has been described as "Italo-Byzantine", but its indebtedness extended to Spain and the Moors, the Pre-Raphaelites and the Symbolists, as well as to Slavonic and Syrian sources. I would describe him primarily as a Baroque artist. He was Baroque in the sensual and ecstatic element in his work, in the carefully pondered way that everything he did was part of the whole scheme to which it contributed, and in a sort of magnificence which redeems the staginess and indifferent drawing of so many compositions. In a way, it is a pity that he was such an effective designer for the theatre, for the very qualities that fitted him for secular drama disqualified him for religious art. His Christs are juvenile leads, his Madonnas are film stars, his angels and saints are a corps de ballet, David is a pantomine king and Solomon belongs to the Ballets Russes. There was something of the Renaissance *uomo universale* about him. Painter, mosaicist and stained glass artist, he was interested in theology, the liturgy, the classics, poetry and history. Of his writings, *Les Entretiens de la Villa du Rouet* and *La Décadence de l'Art Sacré* are probably the best known. Art was for him a reflection of God's splendour and his faith was the light which illuminated all his work. He felt that an artist was participating in the mystery of creation. He worked in pastel, tempera and wax as well as in mosaic and glass, but rarely in oil. It was his aim to "give an artistic future to Switzerland", and it is by the part which he played in the revival of religious art in French Switzerland (a predominantly Calvinist region) that he should be remembered rather than by his own work. He was a great discoverer of other talents, and he encouraged and inspired others without imposing his own ideas on them. Some of his major works may be seen in the churches of Notre-Dame, Geneva; the Cordeliers, Fribourg; Perly, Geneva; the Assumption, Finhaut (Valais); St Martin, Lutry (Vaud); and Sainte-Croix, Carouge, near Geneva.

Another painter who might be described as a Baroque artist born out of due time was Sir Frank Brangwyn (1867–1956). He was greatly admired during his own lifetime, though his rich colour and painterly style made him less popular in England than on the Continent, but he is now almost disregarded. Ripeness is all in his vast mural decorations which sprawl over the interiors of many public buildings, autumnal in tone and thickly populated with figures. He was immensely prolific and a generous donor of his work to Catholic churches. He presented Stations of the Cross to Campion Hall, Oxford, the Benedictine Abbey at Farnborough and to St Wilfred's, Burgess Hill, Sussex. Other examples of his religious work are the painting over the high altar in St Peter's, Morningside, Edinburgh, and windows in the Protestant Cathedral, Belfast. There are Brangwyn Museums in Bruges (his birthplace) and Orange, Vaucluse.

The only important twentieth-century movement which originated outside Paris was Futurism. It is a curious fact that popular opinion seems to regard the term as a synonym for any kind of avant-garde act, and it is therefore necessary to explain its true meaning. On February 20th, 1909, the Italian poet Filippo Tommaso Marinetti wrote an article in *Le Figaro* in which he praised a new kind of beauty—that of machines. The following year a "manifesto of Futurist painting" exalting science, speed and militarism was signed by a group of Italian artists. In many ways, the English movement called Vorticism (*c*. 1914) which revolved around the figure of Percy Wyndham Lewis, was influenced by both Cubism and Futurism although it declared itself anti-Futurist. As machines and speed became commonplace, war a dreadful reality and the surviving Futurists mature men, all the signatories to the Manifesto reverted to more traditional modes of expression. The only Futurist who is important as a religious painter is Gino Severini (b. 1883). He was originally influenced by the Divisionist style of Seurat, and he remained too intellectual an artist to be carried away completely by the sound and fury of Futurism. He was really more attracted by Cubism, and he only used Futurism as an outlet for his impatience with provincial standards in Italy. When he arrived in the more congenial atmosphere of Paris, he no longer felt the need for noisy protests. His compositions became more balanced, his surfaces more serene. His silvery greys and luminous whites are sometimes reminiscent of Braque, and after 1920 he was influenced by Picasso's Pompeiian phase.

Severini has designed mosaics and painted in true fresco in a number of churches, mostly in Switzerland and Italy. His ecclesiastical work, which could be described as Neo-Classical in style, includes a Last Supper in the church of Semsales, Fribourg, and a series of frescoes in the church of Notre-Dame, Lausanne. He has also written several critical works including *Du Cubisme au Classicisme* (1921). Among his characteristic statements one may note: "It is not easy to appreciate a work of art if between it and its appreciation stands a screen of insufficient culture"; and "during the Renaissance art became conscious of its own power, delighting in its own splendour, and this has been the root of all evils from which the modern age is still suffering. Primitive Christian art, on the contrary, whose object was the construction of the work, while the work itself was entirely ordered to the glory of God, is real religious art, illumined with an incomparable purity."

One could wish that other contemporary Italian painters such as Campigli, Sironi, Scipione, and Casorati had produced more religious work. Renato Guttuso (b. 1912), who is usually classified as a social realist, has painted a rather Expressionist Crucifixion with a nude Magdalen.

Dada (which means hobby-horse) was a nonsensical, nihilistic movement of the First World War period which fortunately did not produce any work on religious themes. It has been regarded as a liberating influence, though there were few restraints left from which art needed to be liberated. Its importance was rather in the fact that it led to the more poetic, more mature but almost equally irrational movement called Surrealism, a term evolved by Apollinaire.

By 1922 the wild young men of Dada were a little older

and wiser, and André Breton gathered the survivors into a group devoted to instinctive expression and the interpretation of the unconscious mind. This kind of painting has its roots in the Middle Ages (Hieronymus Bosch) and the Renaissance (Arcimboldi), and there have in fact been few periods in which the weird, the fantastic and the world of dreams have not appealed to artists—Goya, Fuseli and Odilon Redon were other heralds of Surrealism. It is a typically Romantic form of art as may be judged from André Breton's definition in which he said that it was "free from the exercise of reason, and every aesthetic or moral preoccupation". It was the Surrealists who publicized the intrinsic beauty of the *objet trouvé*—the pebble found on the beach, the old tyre on the junk heap, the broken bottle in the gutter. Many important artists were actively connected with the movement, including Giorgio de Chirico, Max Ernst, Marcel Duchamp, René Magritte and Joan Miró. Others, such as Picasso and Sutherland, were influenced in varying degrees. The effect of the movement on sculptors will be mentioned in the appropriate chapter. Salvador Dali (b. 1904) was a leading Surrealist, but although he has painted religious pictures which have achieved wide publicity, he is not to be regarded as a serious artist. The meticulous detail and smooth finish practised by some Surrealists is not a general characteristic. Max Ernst, for instance, had a broader style and made use of *collage* (pieces of paper or fabric stuck on the picture surface) and *frottage* (rubbings taken from some material with an interesting texture).

Marc Chagall (b. 1887) probably influenced the Surrealists, but his fantasies are really of quite a different order. They are strange but not weird or sinister and his imagery has a note of lyrical innocence. His cows can jump over the moon and we find it quite credible: it was probably an everyday occurrence in the Russian-Jewish dreamworld of his childhood. His background was deeply religious and there is a strong emotional appeal in his biblical illustrations and his designs for stained glass. His colours are almost as guileless as Fra Angelico's and his textures often have a kind of bloom like flower petals or a butterfly's wings; but in spite of their beauty, which is in itself spiritually uplifting, his religious works rarely transcend folklore. His biblical illustrations often seem to have strayed from a book of fairy tales or designs for ballet, and his Jerusalem windows from a child's Book of Beasts.

When we turn to the work of Stanley Spencer (1892–1959) we are still in the realm of fantastic imagination, but the level is that of the psychoanalyst's notebook rather than that of nursery rhymes. Stanley Spencer was the most interesting and original religious painter of Protestant background since Blake. Like Blake he was unorthodox, and to many people his iconography was even less comprehensible than Blake's. His "Angels of the Apocalypse" are comic charwomen blown into the sky by some freak whirlwind: his "Christ in the Wilderness" is a hobo who has not so much grown a beard as neglected to shave: his "St Francis with the Birds" is wearing one of his hands back to front and an old dressing gown belonging to Spencer *père*. In spite of these incongruities there is a more powerful religious feeling in these paintings than in those of any of his contemporaries except Rouault.

Spencer's mother attended a Wesleyan chapel but his father was organist at an Anglican church. Stanley himself was deeply responsive to music, and while still a boy said that Bach's St Anne Prelude and Fugue reminded him of "angels shrieking for joy". At first his own faith seems to have been of a simple nonconformist kind, but war service and matrimonial complications changed him and his ideas became increasingly aberrant. In quite a different way from D. H. Lawrence and without abandoning Christianity, he came to regard sex as a sort of religion. Rachel Westropp (wife of the vicar of his native village of Cookham, who had many talks with him during his last illness) said that although his ideas were "far from orthodox" he seemed to believe in the divinity of Christ. He painted huge compositions of the Resurrection and of Christ preaching (which he did not live to finish), localized in the Berkshire village which was to him an earthly paradise. The clumsy figures with which his scenes were peopled were dressed in a bizarre style of supposedly contemporary costume, often covered with hideous patterns. His figure compositions were, not altogether surprisingly, unacceptable to many collectors who clamoured for the landscapes and still lifes which he could turn out in a week or ten days. His pictures of Cookham and its neighbourhood have something of the affectionate description one finds in Pre-Raphaelite painting, and he was a fine though almost conventional portrait painter; but in his visionary work he holds an isolated position, nearer in feeling to the Middle Ages than to the twentieth century. He has been compared with Masaccio, but the darker side of Breughel and Bosch were never very far from the surface. Lady Rothenstein in her sympathetic and penetrating study of him says that he had the nature of a medieval craftsman and village boy. He was completely lacking in the quality which we call style and as far as he was concerned the School of Paris might not have existed. His major work was the mural decoration of Burghclere Chapel in Berkshire, with its altar-piece of "The Resurrection of the Soldiers".

Another visionary painter, though not of the same stature, is Cecil Collins (b. 1908). His work was shown in the International Surrealist Exhibition in London in 1936, but he is nearer to the Symbolists, particularly Odilon Redon, than to the main stream of Surrealism. His work is not irrational for his intellect is at least as much involved as his impulses. His style is calligraphic, his colour has been described as heraldic, and many of his pictures have some of the qualities of a Byzantine icon; for instance, the apostles in an *Agony in the Garden* (Collection of Peter Pears) assumes attitudes related to those used by generations of icon painters. He has no patience with "pure painting" which he regards as "visual confectionery". To him, colours and forms are instruments, and painting a metaphysical activity. He has a recurring image of the Fool, wiser than the worldlings and, like his dancing angels, full of spiritual joy. Although his work is in many public and private collections, Cecil Collins seems to have been neglected by ecclesiastical patrons. Apart from his paintings, he has designed fine fabrics and tapestries which could well be used in churches.

The term *École de Paris* is a vague one covering many of the international movements of the first half of the twentieth century, and meaning little more than the pre-eminence of Paris as a powerhouse of artistic activity during this period. In earlier times, as we have seen, artists flocked to Rome; and in the nineteen fifties, with the spread of abstract art, the emphasis began to shift to New York.

David Jones (b. 1895) could scarcely avoid being influenced by current idioms, but with a kind of inspired selectivity he only absorbed as much as was good for him. His art is in many ways unique, and at the same time peculiarly English. He himself is very consciously Welsh, but there has been nothing quite like his work since Anglo-Saxon times. By this I do not mean to imply that he is archaistic, but he has the same tenuous line, as fine as a cobweb but as strong as steel, and the same rain-washed colour, that we find in the Caedmon manuscript. In my opinion, his water colours are the most sensitive and exquisite in twentieth-century art. Unfortunately, they do not reproduce well, and when subjected to printing processes they fade like flowers in a drought or delicate wine that has been handled carelessly. For this reason a wood-engraving which the artist considers to be his best, has been chosen to illustrate this book. It was during the fruitful period of his association with Eric Gill at Ditchling not long after he became a Catholic, that David Jones learned the craft of engraving. At the same time he read and was greatly impressed by Maritain's *Art et Scholastique*.[1] He left behind at Ditchling some paintings on walls and panels which, being in an opaque medium, are broader but less fluent and nervous in handling than those which we regard as characteristic. Their relationship with the engravings is, however, obvious. One of these (an Entry into Jerusalem called *Cum Floribus et Palmis*) which was painted without any proper preparation on a brick wall, has now disappeared; a Crucifixion and a Flagellation can still be seen in the chapel of the Guild of St Joseph and St Dominic. Although much of David Jones's work can be called religious in a wider sense, his illustrations for the *Chester Play of the Deluge* (published by the Golden Cockerel Press) are perhaps the most important on specifically Christian themes.

Another graphic artist, also a mural painter, who should be remembered is Thomas Derrick (1885–1954).

Jean Cocteau (1891–1963) was a brilliant and versatile figure, more notable for his contribution to literature and entertainment than for his talents in the visual arts; but he should be remembered for his work in restoring the Fishermen's Chapel at Villefranche-sur-Mer, Alpes-Maritimes. The result, like Matisse's Chapelle du Rosaire at Vence, has some of the elements of stage scenery as well as the same virtue of unity. The decoration incorporates a mural of the Miraculous Draught of Fishes and the motif of the Eye traditionally painted on fishing boats.

During the 1950's painting became increasingly abstract, although there are signs of a return to representation in such movements as "pop art" and "la nouvelle figuration". It should no longer be necessary to defend the principles of

[1] English translation *Art and Scholasticism*, London and New York, Sheed and Ward, 1938.

abstract art; but I think that usage is a more important justification than the much-quoted passage in Plato's *Philebus* about the permanent and natural and absolute beauty of "straight lines and curves, or the surfaces or solid forms produced out of these. . . ." No one questions the validity of the Greek fret, the pattern on a Persian carpet, or the sett of the McGillivray tartan; and although abstract painting as such has not been much employed in ecclesiastical commissions, abstract design has been readily assimilated into such crafts as stained glass, ceramics, mosaic and textiles, all of which will be referred to in the appropriate chapter. In fact, a grave menace has arisen in the shape of a new kind of abstract *bondieuserie*, particularly in France: for patrons not sufficiently expert to judge the merits of modern representational art have tended to take refuge in abstraction, which seems to them to combine in a convenient way the qualities of safety, "good taste" and modernity. Often the abstract work is feeble in the extreme and fails not only as design but also as a means of communication. This lack of communication is one of the difficulties associated with abstract religious art. It cannot, of course, be didactic, but few would wish religious art to be didactic today. It can suggest or even induce an emotion, a mood or a frame of mind, though everyone may not react to the same work in the same way. This element has always existed in the use of colours and shapes which are in themselves evocative.

The chief danger in abstract painting is that below the level of artists such as Tobey, Rothko, Poliakoff or Ben Nicholson, painters as well as patrons are inclined to regard it as an easy solution to the present crisis in art; and although a bad abstract painting may win acceptance because it seems in keeping with modern buildings, it can be just as insincere as a piece of sentimental nineteenth-century realism, without being half so workmanlike. Fr Cocagnac, O.P., has drawn a distinction between art which retains some respect for form and balance (even if it is only transfigured form or a mere spectre of form) and Action Painting which seems to him to be too self-centred. Although it is difficult to define the quality that makes an abstract work Christian it is nevertheless recognizable. It can express unmistakably such ideas as transcendence, immanence, infinity and sacred mystery. Among the artists who have produced work of this kind are Alfred Manessier (b. 1911), Jean-René Bazaine (b. 1904), Raoul Ubac (b. 1910) and, in a very different style, the young Australian painter Leonard French (b. 1928). Manessier has said that figurative art is a Promised Land to which sacred art will at length find the right path after wandering in the wilderness, and that when it arrives it will be enriched by the discoveries of contemporary art.

CHAPTER VI

TWO CENTURIES OF CHRISTIAN SCULPTURE

The ecstasy and agitation of Baroque and Rococo seem to have left sculpture drained of vitality. The period with which we have to deal is one of the least inspiring in the history of religious art. The most renowned artists were employed in designing elaborate tombs, public statues and portrait busts of great technical skill but little aesthetic validity. Although Neo-Classic sculptors paid lip-service to Greece, their models were more often tired Hellenistic works or second-rate copies excavated in Italy. Their nostalgia for the past, even though it was a classical past, was in itself Romantic. The Greeks to them seemed simple and unspoiled compared with the Romans, and they imagined Greek art (as they imagined Gothic art) to be almost primitive. This attitude often lent their work a sentimental quality which was quite remote from anything in genuine Greek art, and when the Elgin marbles were first seen in Western Europe they were regarded by many as inferior to the Apollo Belvedere.

Jean-Antoine Houdon (1741–1828) enjoyed the greatest reputation among French sculptors of the eighteenth century. Although his active career falls largely outside our period and was more productive of portrait busts than of religious work, he is of interest because he carried out an ecclesiastical commission which was perhaps the first to dispense with Baroque gesture and rhetoric. This was the colossal statue of St Bruno in marble, made in 1764 for the Roman church of Santa Maria degli Angeli. Referring to the fact that St Bruno was the founder of the Carthusians, the pope said when he saw it: "He would speak if his Order did not forbid it!" The statue is, in fact, calm, simple and classical, and no doubt the quiet nobility of gesture seemed unusually natural to the pope after the theatrical attitudes to which he was accustomed. The fact that Houdon made one statue of Washington (now at Richmond, Va) and Canova another (in the State Capitol) no doubt contributed to the realistic and Neo-Classical tendencies in American sculpture which survived almost until the end of the nineteenth century.

Antonio Canova (1757–1822) was the most celebrated sculptor of his time in Europe. He was trained as a mason and although the more animated and naturalistic style of his youth (which had its roots in Rococo) set into a typically Neo-Classic mould, it was saved from the lifelessness of some of his contemporaries by his refusal to leave everything except the design to his assistants. Before they were allowed to help with any of his commissions, his apprentices were obliged to spend a year in a stone quarry "to get the feel of stone", and he always worked with full-sized models to preserve a sense of scale and to retain the sensitivity of the original modelling. Many of his admirers thought him greater than Michelangelo. His first major commission was the monument to Pope Clement XIV (1782–7) followed by that to Clement XIII (1787–92). The monument to Maria Cristina in the Augustinerkirche, Vienna, is also his work. After the fall of Napoleon he was instrumental in negotiating the return of many of the works of art looted from Italy by the French. For this the pope created him Marchese d'Ischia. At the expense of George III he made the Stuart Monument which is now in St Peter's. In addition he was responsible for a number of large ecclesiastical paintings.

Canova was an extremely sympathetic character, apparently devoid of professional jealousy. He was always ready to help students and impecunious artists with money and commissions. When he first saw the Elgin Marbles he was humble enough to exclaim: "Oh that I had but to begin again! To unlearn all I have learned! I now see what ought to form the real school of sculpture."

One of the young artists whom Canova welcomed to Rome in his usual kindly way and took into his studio was Bertel Thorwaldsen (1768–1844). Rome was then, as it remained until the middle of the nineteenth century, the Mecca of sculptors. It should be mentioned that the accessibility of so many works of antiquity was largely due to the eighteenth-century popes, whose contribution to the arts is less widely acknowledged than that of their Renaissance predecessors. Clement XI (1700–21) insisted that all archeological discoveries should be reported to the Commissioner of Antiquities and recorded in engravings. He improved the arrangement of classical sculpture in the Vatican and laid the foundations of the Museum of Christian Antiquities. Clement XII (1730–40) opened what must have been the first public Museum of Antiquities in Europe. Benedict XIV (1740–58), besides adding extensively to the collections, had catalogues made and encouraged artists and students in many ways. He also enlarged the Museum of Christian Antiquities. Clement XIII (1758–69) though he has been criticized for covering statues which seemed to him indecent, was the patron of Mengs and Piranesi and carried on the tradition of conservation and collection. It was he who appointed Winckelmann as Commissioner of Antiquities. Work of extension continued under Clement XIV (1769–75) and Pius VI (1775–1800) by which time the Vatican had attained to its present position of the most important Museum of Antiquities in the world. When Thorwaldsen saw these splendours he declared that he had not been born until he came to Rome; but it is hard nowadays to understand the esteem in which he was held, for his work seems insipid, cold and derivative. Much of it was the work of assistants, for he only made the models and added the finishing touches. He was lazy, grasping and unreliable, and some scandal was caused by his being given commissions for the tomb of Pius VII and for a colossal group of Christ and the Apostles for a Protestant church in Copenhagen: for it was said that, although nominally a Protestant, his morals and religious beliefs were not above reproach. However, his patrons quite rightly thought that the quality of his work was the only criterion which need concern them, and Thorwaldsen was considered, however mistakenly, the best sculptor available.

John Flaxman (1755–1826) was one of the few English artists to achieve an international reputation, though it was his beautiful and vigorous drawing (book illustrations for Homer, Aeschylus, Hesiod and Dante) rather than his sculpture, which was so widely influential. He had great powers of invention and design, and a linear rhythm which one recognizes as peculiarly English. His talents were better adapted to relief than to sculpture in the round. He had a firm belief in the high moral value of art, and having seen that "the mistress to whom great artists of Italy had dedicated their genius was the Church", he conceived the idea of "serving the Protestant Church by a far different application of the resources of art". He could not, however, escape the influence of what he had seen in Rome, and some of his monuments reflect the style of the seventeenth-century papal tombs; others have angels derived from his drawings of Trecento subjects, while those of Agnes Cromwell in Chichester Cathedral and Mrs Morley in Gloucester Cathedral seem to have been adapted partly from Bacchic reliefs and partly from representations of the Assumption. He liked to use biblical texts on his monuments, and although his religious symbolism is non-committal, it is much more

Christian in feeling than that of John Bacon (1740–99) who was a pillar of the Methodist Church, or Thomas Banks (1735–1805) who was said to be an unbeliever, though his daughter described him as a Dissenter. Flaxman had a considerable influence on the Nazarenes and on Ingres, and he was friendly with Blake who addressed him as "Dear Sculptor of Eternity". It was probably Blake who inspired his sympathy with medieval art and his interest in Swedenborg, but he always remained a Low Churchman. His most important statue of a religious subject is the "St Michael overcoming Satan" at Petworth.

John Bacon had been responsible for introducing better pointing equipment for transferring the clay model to the marble, as a result of which more and more work was left to assistants. By 1800, very little work on the final stone was done by the master himself, except in the case of Canova: and even he, when his practice had grown very large, must have delegated most of the actual carving. Some of Flaxman's work suffers from the fact that he usually made a small model which, when enlarged by the mason, lost much of its sensitivity.

Sir Francis Chantry (1781–1841) did not exactly contribute to the history of religious art, but he evolved a new style of tomb sculpture for bishops, in which he specialized. Instead of a recumbent effigy he carved a figure in prayer which, although it seems unremarkable now, was then considered quite revolutionary. The most romantic piece of religious sculpture produced during this period was the bronze "Joan of Arc in Prayer" (Musée Des Beaux Arts, Orléans) by Princess Marie d'Orléans, Duchess of Württemburg (1813–39). It is unusual for a royal princess to make a serious study of art—Louise Hollandine, daughter of the Winter Queen, is another example. Princess Marie was taught by Baron de Triquetti, but may also have been given lessons by Barye, who was working for the royal family at the time.

The realistic trend continued in France with François Rude (1784–1855), J. B. Carpeaux (1827–75) and Jules Dalou (1838–1902), all of whom had an influence in England. In the United States sculptors modelled themselves on Flaxman and Thorwaldsen until after the Civil War, when the great American collections began to be built up, providing artists with new sources of inspiration. Everywhere religious sculpture was characterized by a sentimental plastic realism and the sort of works that were admired were the simpering "Virgin with a Lily" or "St Agnes" by Eugène Delaplanche (1836–91) and the banal "Christian Martyr" or "St Vincent de Paul" by Alexandre Falguière (1831–1900).

It was perhaps in Italy that religious sculpture sank to its lowest depths, and all that can be said in its favour is that its practitioners relied less on the pointing machine and carved their monstrosities with their own hands. Elsewhere, in the second half of the nineteenth century, it was almost unheard of for a sculptor to do any of the final carvings himself, and Ruskin was considered revolutionary when he wrote in 1870:

> The modern system of modelling the work in clay: getting it into form by machinery and by the hands of subordinates; and touching it at last if indeed the (so-called) sculptor touches it at all, only to correct their inefficiencies, renders the production of good work in marble or stone a physical impossibility. The first result is that the sculptor thinks in clay instead of marble. . . . The second is that neither he nor the public recognize the touch of the chisel as expressive of personal feeling or power, and that nothing is looked for except mechanical polish.

The outstanding figure of late nineteenth-century sculpture was Auguste Rodin (1840–1917). Although he was as much in revolt against academism as the Impressionists, he continued the practice of employing an army of masons and makers of casts, and he completely ignored the character of his materials. He infused his work with a sort of super-charged realism; his power of observation was outstanding, his anatomical knowledge precise and his dynamic force undeniable; but he was limited by his lack of intellect and discipline and everything that he did was conceived in clay. His output was enormous, but although he produced some Christian subjects, they do not express any religious feeling. One suspects that the "Prodigal Son" and "St John the Baptist Preaching" are just convenient titles for nude male figures in action. He was both adulated and execrated by his contemporaries, some of whom equated him with Pheidias, Donatello and Michelangelo, while others attacked his work with choppers as well as with words.

Antoine Bourdelle (1861–1929) worked for a long time in Rodin's studio and was unable at first to break away from fluid handling and plastic surfaces; but he sought inspiration in archaic Greek, ancient Egyptian and Gothic art, and eventually achieved a more glyptic feeling. His "Virgin of Alsace" has a simple monumental quality suited to its dominant site on one of the summits of the Vosges, and Maurice Denis called it: "A masterpiece of modern art and of religious art of all time." Bourdelle was influential as a teacher among those who reacted against Rodin's lack of respect for his materials.

Ivan Mestrovic (b. 1883) and Eric Gill (1882–1940) were the first sculptors of any importance for many years to de-vote a large proportion of their work to Christian themes. Mestrovic is a very uneven artist, perhaps because he has worked in a wide range of media which are not equally suited to his talents; these include wood, plaster, marble and bronze, and his commissions have included portraits, public monuments and nudes as well as ecclesiastical work. He has been responsible for memorial chapels in his native Yugo-slavia and has made an over life-size crucifix in oak for the

Church of the Holy Cross at Split. This last work is rather Expressionist in feeling and is less successful than his more rhythmic and less angular carvings in wood, such as the "Lamentation over the Dead Christ" (usually described as a Deposition) in the Tate Gallery, which contains echoes of Dalmatia's Byzantine past. Important exhibitions of his work in Rome (1911) and London (1915) won him recognition in Europe and America. He accepted a professorial appointment in the University of Syracuse (New York) in 1947.

Eric Gill could carve inscriptions as noble as any in ancient Rome, and the alphabets which he designed bear comparison with those of the Renaissance masters; but as a figurative sculptor he was limited, particularly in his religious works. This may have been partly due to his obsession with the physical act of carving, and to the blunting of his imagination by his rather cranky refusal to admit that there was any more in art than honest craftsmanship and a sense of responsibility. When he was carving an inscription he was doing a straightforward job of work at which he must have known that he was unrivalled; but when he embarked on a piece of figurative sculpture theories became entangled between his mind, his hand and his material. This was less noticeable in his torsos (such as "Mankind" in the Tate Gallery) which are the most masterly as well as the most classical of his figurative carvings; they are relaxed and assured and convey a delight in execution which is only equalled by his beautiful drawings of nudes. In comparison, his religious work nearly always looks cramped and stammering, as though it had been executed by a man who was bound and gagged. This may have been partly due to the fact that he never really succeeded in reconciling his sensuality with his Christianity. He made a great parade of it instead of accepting it as part of his nature, and perhaps because he felt that his faith put some sort of brake on his eroticism, he unconsciously expressed this restraint in his religious work. This did not prevent it from being an advance on anything else being done at that time in England. He had a magnetic personality which attracted a number of disciples who regarded him as a kind of sage, a rôle which he adopted readily enough. He was a born preacher who was able to make a convincing digest of the ideas embodied in the writings of Maritain (and ultimately in scholastic philosophy), Coomeraswamy and W. R. Lethaby, to whom he did not always make due acknowledgement. It is largely to him that we owe the discredit of the pointing machine, and the return to direct carving. His condemnation of modelling as a prelude to carving was so violent that he and his followers were almost inclined to question the validity of modelling as an art form in its own right, although it has a history as venerable as glyptic sculpture and has produced works no less beautiful and noble.

Those who learned their craft from Eric Gill attained a skill almost indistinguishable from his own, and in true workshop tradition they were allowed to make their own contribution to his commissions; but they tended to repeat his more tiresome mannerisms or weaknesses—the dreadful sawdust-doll legs, the archaistic wry necks and other arthritic attitudes. If any of his students (among whom Anthony Foster, who died at the age of forty-seven in 1957, was one of the best) had been of sufficient stature he might have started a worthy school of sculpture; for when an artist of real quality, such as David Jones, came under his influence, the result was rewarding. There can be little doubt that the discipline of workshop practice gave the intensely personal art of David Jones a new conviction and sense of direction.

Among Eric Gill's more important religious sculpture may be included the Stations of the Cross at Westminster Cathedral and St Cuthbert's Church, Bradford: the "Creation of Adam" at Geneva: and the relief of "Christ driving the Money-Changers from the Temple" at Leeds University. His major work in wood is the altar-piece for Rossall School chapel, and his own favourite carving was the "Deposition" now at King's School, Canterbury. He was also, of course, a prolific graphic artist, in which medium his masterpiece is the series of wood engravings made to illustrate the *Four Gospels* published by the Golden Cockerel Press. His respect for the medium in which he was working was such that whether he was using stone, wood, or a common lead pencil, he never tried to make his materials do anything that was out of character.

Sir Jacob Epstein (1880–1959) was in several respects something of a phenomenon. His work, while never arousing the passions of real connoisseurs, continued throughout his career to excite public opinion to fever pitch. His carved sculpture, in which he adopted some of the conventions of primitive art, was always calculated to cause a scandal or an outcry. It was tarred and feathered, attacked from pulpits and in newspapers, and defended with equal fervour. His bronzes, however, reminiscent of Rodin in the fluidity of their modelling but even more shaggy of surface, were immensely popular; they had a kind of brutal vitality and his portrait busts often achieved a likeness which, without exactly flattering the sitter, endowed him with a rugged potency that was usually much larger than life. Epstein's style scarcely changed or developed from his student days to the end of his life. He made a brief excursion into Vorticism, and his method of carving benefited by a period of working with Eric Gill; but it would be difficult to date most of his bronzes on internal evidence for they are all conceived as clay, they are all restless, and they all have the look of victims, as though their creator has taken a sadistic pleasure in gouging out their eyes and tangling their hair.

Although a Jew, and although his work was sometimes condemned as obscene or blasphemous, Epstein was entrusted with several important ecclesiastical commissions. Towards the end of his career he used other metals as well as bronze, and his works in lead and aluminium are perhaps to be preferred. The Madonna and Child at the Holy Child Convent, Cavendish Square, London, vibrates with feeling but dangles rather aimlessly on its supporting wall. The Satan at Coventry is merely nasty and no match for an archangel.

Henry Moore (b. 1898) is probably the first English sculptor since Flaxman to occupy a position of international eminence. Although his religious works are rare, they are excellent examples of the way in which a good artist can with proper humility adapt himself to the needs of a client without losing any of his own integrity. There are those who think that Henry Moore's Madonnas are not so deeply felt as some of the subjects which are of his own choosing; but he approached the work in the right spirit, recognizing that here was something more than a mere mother-and-child image, and the result is simple, moving and, like all his work, truly monumental. Henry Moore's outlook is very different from Eric Gill's, although the older man admired his work, and encouraged him. He is much less concerned with the physical act of carving and holds the more conventional view that the most vital part of an artist's function is the conception of the work, not its execution. One might over-simplify the position by saying that whereas Eric Gill would have been inclined to think that a piece of sculpture, carried out with skill, honesty and due consideration for the material and for its ultimate purpose, was bound to be right aesthetically, Henry Moore would be inclined to think that if the imaginative power motivating the act of creation had sufficient drive, it ought to surmount any problems of execution. His respect for the medium almost amounts to obsequiousness when he allows the character of the stone to dictate what form the sculpture shall take. This is why so many of his works look like natural phenomena produced by erosion or other elemental forces. In this sense they could be called more naturalistic than those of any "photographic" artist.

Among English sculptors who have been influenced by Moore rather than Gill, Arthur Pollen (b. 1899) has some claim to distinction in the sphere of religious art, although he is an uneven artist who has not succeeded in resolving all his problems. His natural bent is Classical, or perhaps one should say Pre-Classical, and he is at his best when he wraps his figures in formalized draperies from Leonidan Sparta, gives his Christ a head from a red figure vase and his Virgin a Phrygian cap. When he works against this grain, the result usually lacks conviction. Among his more important religious works may be included the crucifix with clothed figure on the exterior of the Catholic Church at Hurst Green, Sussex: the crucifix in a private chapel of Farm Street Church, London: and the gilt-bronze statue of St Patrick in Westminster Cathedral.

Philip Lindsey Clark (b. 1889) is a sort of elder statesman among English religious sculptors, for apart from Eric Gill he was for a long time the only standard bearer for something more worthy of a place in churches than the mechanical statuary of Italian masons. The most enduring source of his inspiration seems to have been the earlier work at Chartres, but there is less tension in his figures and his drapery is less nervous. When carving wood or working in bronze he allows himself more movement. His work is to be found in many parts of the British Isles, notably in Westminster Cathedral, Aylesford and Hawkesyard Priories, the Church of the English Martyrs, Wallasey, and St Mary's, Cadogan Street, Chelsea. Among those who learned their craft from him, Peter Watts (b. 1916) has achieved a wide reputation on both sides of the Atlantic. Michael Clark (b. 1916) carries on the family tradition—for his grandfather too was a sculptor

—in quite a different idiom. His work, of which typical examples may be seen at Aylesford Priory and the Catholic Church at Midhurst, Sussex, is neither austere nor much stylized, but human and lively; without making too many concessions to popular taste, he has achieved something which is "understanded of the people". He may be contrasted with Josephina de Vasconcellos who has compromised too much, so that her Virgin and Child groups for St Paul's Cathedral and St James's, Piccadilly, and her Nativity for St Martin-in-the-Fields (all in London) are merely pretty. Another woman sculptor who has carried out many ecclesiastical commissions is Julian Allan (b. 1892).

In the first half of the twentieth century the three most prominent names in German sculpture were Lehmbruch, Kolbe and Barlach. Of these, Ernst Barlach (1870–1938) was the most Christian in subject-matter. He was an Expressionist of great power with something reminiscent of late Gothic both in his feeling and in his method of woodcarving, in which the toolmarks sometimes seem rather arbitrary. He carved the angel hovering over the War Memorial in the Antoniterkirche, Alstadt, Cologne, and a crucifix in St Elizabeth's, Marburg. Among living German artists who have produced worthwhile sculpture one must number Hilde Schurk-Frisch. Her work varies in quality but is sometimes very telling, especially in representations of the Madonna and Child in which the Child is often intimately connected with the Mother as though not yet accustomed to a separate existence. Her figures often dwell on the action of listening or being open to the Voice or Will of God (e.g. St Joseph in the church of Essen-Bredeney and the bronze angel in the concert-hall of the Castle of Ahaus). Siegfried Charoux, born in Austria in 1896, came to England as a refugee and has carried out a number of official commissions in this country. His religious work includes a Madonna and Child at Pinner, Middlesex.

In France and Belgium during the same period none of the sculptors engaged on ecclesiastical work was equal in stature to Aristide Maillol (1861–1944), whose œuvre consisted almost entirely of splendid, innocent, healthy female nudes. Maillol was a close friend of Maurice Denis, and one regrets that the painter did not persuade the sculptor to use his abundant talent in the service of the Church. Ossip Zadkine was born in Russia in 1890, but studied in England and France and has lived in Paris since 1909, so he may be considered here. There is a Baroque, almost Rococo, quality in his pyramidal groupings of forms and a vein of lyrical fantasy in his mode of expression. His feeling for religious drama has been realized in such subjects as a Pietà, the Good Samaritan and two versions of the Prodigal Son. When I last saw these works, in 1961, they were still in the possession of the artist. Henri Charlier has been described as "a sort of Christian Maillol" and "a Fra Angelico among sculptors", but although his carving is honest and craftsmanlike and no doubt looked very simple and direct against the routine work of thirty years ago, it now seems respectable but dull. He has carved a whole series of capitals for the church of St Joseph at La Bourboule, where the extensive iconographic scheme recalls the great ensembles of the Middle Ages—Old Testament subjects, types of Christ, the hidden life of Nazareth and subjects related to the Eucharist such as Melchisedech, the gathering of manna, and the disciples going to Emmaus. He has made statues of our Lady of Lourdes and St Bernadette for the chapel of St Bernadette at Montpelier, and a slightly polychromed Virgin and Child for the Abbey Church of St André-lez-Bruges.

In Switzerland, François Baud (b. 1889) was the first modern sculptor of religious subjects. He mourned the decay of the workshop system and would probably have applauded Samuel Butler's dictum: "An art can only be

1. The Adoration of the Kings, by William Blake, 1799

2. Holy Family in a German Landscape, by Ferdinand Von Olivier, 1824. The scene can be identified as a sandpit near Vienna

3. Churches built in Bethnal Green during the 1840's

4. The Triumph of the Innocents, by William Holman Hunt, 1884. Tate Gallery, London

5. Church of the Annunciation, Brighton. Window designed by Burne-Jones and Rossetti and made by William Morris, 1865

6. Sagrada Familia, Barcelona, Antonio Gaudí (1883–1926). Nativity façade

7. Holy Water Stoup, by Gaudí. Church of Santa Coloma, nr. Barcelona

8. Chalice by Henry Wilson, 1898. Silver gilt repoussé, appliqués cast and chased, blue and green enamel knop, carved ivory decoration St Bartholomew's, Brighton

9. The Visitation, ceramic panel by Teresa Fuller. Digby Stuart College, London

10. Lamentation over the Dead Christ, wood panel by Ivan Mestrovic, 1917. Tate Gallery, London

11. The Bride, wood engraving by David Jones, 1930

12. Study for Zacharias and Elizabeth, by Stanley Spencer, pencil and sepia wash, 1912

13. Christ and the Money Changers, by Eric Gill. The University of Leeds

14. Notre Dame, Le Raincy, Auguste Perret, 1922–3

15. Madonna and Child (detail), by Henry Moore. Church of St Matthew, Northampton

16. Madonna and Child, by Arthur Pollen, 1948

17. Madonna and Child, by Jacob Epstein. Convent of H.C.J., London.

18. Detail from gold chalice by Dunstan Pruden, 1959. Cathedral of Christ the King, Liverpool

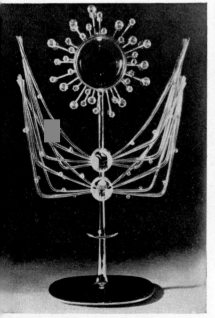

20. The Beatitudes, by Evie Hone

19. Monstrance, by Meinrad Burch-Korrodi, 1953. Silver gilt, rock crystal and enamel

21. Sainte Marie de la Tourette, Le Corbusier, 1960. The 'canons à lumière' can be seen on the left

23. Saint-Rémy, Baccarat, Nicolas Kazis, 1957

22. St Anna, Düren, Rudolf Schwartz, 1956

24. Reformed Church, Aerdenhout, Holland, Karel L. Sijmons, 1958

25. Windows in Oundle School Chapel, designed by John Piper and executed by Patrick Reyntiens, 1956–7; l. to r.: The Light, the Way, the Truth

26. Chasuble in spun silk, white with gold stripe, made by Valentine KilBride, 1957

27. Handwoven black silk chasuble made by the Benedictine monks of Montserrat, Spain, 1964

28. Abbey Church of St John, Collegeville, Minnesota, designed by Marcel Breuer, 1953–61, Bell banner, North façade

29. Collegeville. Sanctuary

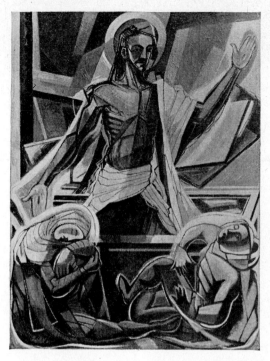

30. The Resurrection, by Roy de Maistre

31. John the Baptist, by Francis Souza, 1963

32. Head of Christ, study for the Coventry tapestry by Graham Sutherland, 1960

33. The Baptism of Christ, by Bernard Buffet. Château l'Arc, nr. Aix-en-Provence

35. Daughters of Jerusalem, detail of ceramic Stations of the Cross, by Adam Kossowski. Church of St Ambrose, Speke, Liverpool

34. The Marriage Feast at Cana, by Fernand Léger

36. Christ Church, Bochum, Germany, designed by Dieter Oesterlen, windows by Helmut Lander, 1957

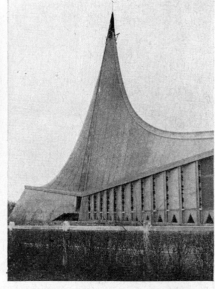

37 & 38. Saint-Thibaut, Marly-le-Roi, France. Architects Perrouin, Lunel and Yung, windows by Maurice Rocher, 1962–5. The wooden vault and the exterior

39. La Sainte Face, by Georges Rouault, 1933. Musée National d'Art Moderne, Paris

learned in the workshop of those who are winning their bread by it." Baud complained that without a band of assistants trained in the master's ways, it was impossible to carry out ensembles of the kind which contributed to the unity of medieval or even Renaissance churches. However, he did succeed, with the help of Charles Collet (b. 1902), in completing a scheme of this kind in the Church of St Joseph at Geneva (1939). The series of stone capitals there, his most important work, represent scenes from the Old Testament, and reveal the influences of a year's stay in Indo-China. He also worked in wood, bronze and ceramics. Charles Collet independently carved capitals in the monastery of Montserrat, and made statues for many Spanish churches. Albert Schilling represents a more advanced and interesting school in Switzerland. Although he has been responsible for a number of statues (for example, Notre-Dame de la Trinité in All Saints, Basle), his name has been associated particularly with altars, tabernacles and fonts. If present liturgical trends continue, it seems probable that we shall see fewer tabernacles, but where they are still customary or obligatory, Albert Schilling's are as good as any. He has initiated a type which has been much imitated—a casket form, often in bronze, with lettering or surface decoration. His altars are often very fine. They are usually simple blocks of stone with symbolic reliefs or incised decoration. Sometimes, if the stone or marble has a particularly interesting character of its own, it is left unadorned except perhaps for a few hollows or rectangular spaces suggestive of the entrance to a rupestral tomb. His fonts are not always so successful, as they have a tendency to look like gigantic ashtrays.

Among the older generation of European sculptors, several have influenced younger artists without having made any notable contributions to Christian art themselves. The Rumanian Constantin Brancusi (1876–1957) was perhaps the most important of these. With his emphasis on ovoid forms, his belief in vertical movement to suggest prayer, a sense of suspension and a detachment that has been described as oriental, he influenced the short-lived Chilean sculptor Juana Müller (1911–52), whose work includes a tabernacle for Notre-Dame en Sainte-Melaine, Rennes. Hans Arp (b. 1887) besides making a baptismal font for the church of All Saints, Basle, has been the god-father of all those organic shapes which seem to change and grow as we look at them, and of those overlapping or inter-secting forms like clouds or birds with heads tucked under their wings. Julio Gonzalez (1876–1942), the Catalan sculptor, made a profound impression on young English and American sculptors with his work in wrought iron. In America, Carl Milles (1875–1955), Swedish by birth, enjoyed the greatest reputation of any sculptor since Rodin, who influenced him in his youth; but Milles had much more feeling for sculpture in an architectural setting, and a more rhythmic and lyrical sense of design. William Zorach (b. 1887 in Lithuania) also won a high reputation and his porphyry head of Christ in the Museum of Modern Art, New York, is worthy of mention.

There are many artists of the first rank whose work could well be used for ecclesiastical purposes if someone had the imagination to commission them. Why not a mobile by Alexander Calder (b. 1898) on a church roof? Why not two beasts by Lynn Chadwick (b. 1914) to guard the church door, like the lions at so many medieval Italian porches? Why not a set of Stations of the Cross (if one must have more than simple crosses) by Ralph Brown (b. 1928)? A place could also be found for the beautiful transparent construc-tions of artists such as George Vantongerloo (b. 1886), Naum Gabo (b. 1890), his brother Antoine Pevsner (1886–1962) and Lazlo Moholy-Nagy (b. 1895). Some sculptors of international reputation have, of course, been given important commissions, notably Giacomo Manzù (b. 1908) for new doors of St Peter's, Rome (1950) and Salzburg Cathedral (1958) and for a relief of St Teresa of Lisieux in Westminster Cathedral; Ewald Mataké (1887–1965) also made bronze doors for Cologne and Salzburg Cathedrals and for The World Peace Church at Hiroshima; and Germaine Richier (1904–59), whose disintegrated surfaces and fractured masses seem so remote from the influence of her master Bourdelle, was one of the many famous names associated with the church of Notre-Dame de Toutes Grâces at Assy. Jacques Lipschitz was another, and a figure of Christ by Germaine Richier can also be seen in the Church of Saint-Jean-Baptiste, Breteuil, Oise.

Since earliest times, sculpture has been divided into two opposed but equally traditional methods. Glyptic sculpture, in which the inner form is released by carving from without, is a process of attrition; modelling, which builds up soft materials from within before firing them in a kiln or making a metal cast from them, is a process of addition. In the last half century, modern technology has added a third method. This is a process of welding, in which rods, bars, and lumps of metal are joined, bent, stretched, thickened and beaten into shape, or sometimes, one might think, into shapelessness. This tends to produce a kind of sculpture in which space is regarded as a negative but important element. There is usually a restlessness and urgency about it which seems typical of current society. Some of its established practitioners such as Reg Butler, Lynn Chadwick and Anthony Caro began in other professions such as architecture and engineering, but others, including Kenneth Armitage, Robert Clatworthy, Hubert Dalwood, Elizabeth Frink, F. E. McWilliam, Bernard Meadows and Eduardo Paolozzi received conventional art school training. There seems to be scope for this kind of sculpture in the attenuated figures needed for altar crucifixes where Mass is said facing the people. These are often made by goldsmiths, for the leading members of this craft, such as Meinrad Burch-Korrodi, Dunstan Pruden, Hein Wimmer and Roger Bonduel, are invariably sculptors: Dunstan Pruden, for instance, also carves in ivory and wood.

Increasing numbers of sculptors on the Continent of Europe are devoting the greater part of their output to work for churches, with varying degrees of success. Those in great demand include (mostly in France) Lambert Rücki (Stations of the Cross at Notre-Dame de la Sainte Trinité, Blois, façade at Saint-Lazare, Chartres) and Pierre Szekely (sculpture and doors at the Hermitage Chapel, Saint-Rouin, and, with Vera Szekely, tabernacle and crucifix at Sainte-Geneviève, Palaiseau): and (mostly in Belgium) Jean Williame (statues at Chapelle de Heer Agimont and the guest chapel of the Abbey of Saint-André, Bruges).

CHAPTER VII

A FANTASTICAL
SPANIARD AND SOME
CONTEMPORARIES

Stylistic changes in architecture sometimes result from new ways of doing and sometimes from new ways of thinking, but usually from a combination of both. The ribbed vault was a dominant factor in the birth of the Gothic style, whereas Renaissance, Baroque and Rococo architecture were much more the outcome of states of mind. Technical developments have played a larger part in nineteenth- and twentieth-century building than in that of any other age, but there was a long period in which the survival of old ideas inhibited the exploitation of new materials and methods.

Iron had been worked industrially since the second half of the eighteenth century, and cast-iron columns, beams and girders had been used in churches since the 1770's (as in St Anne's, Liverpool); but the style of Boileau and Lusson's Saint-Eugène in Paris (1854–5) made no concessions to the fact that it was the first church in which iron was used throughout. It was still Neo-Gothic, and so was the first church in reinforced concrete (de Baudot and Contamin's Saint-Jean in Montmartre, built between 1894 and 1897), although various systems of applying this material had been patented since 1844. Prefabrication was closely associated with iron construction, but ecclesiastical authorities were not impressed by its success in the colonies and the goldfields. John Wallis of London might ship a "do-it-yourself" palace to an African king in 1843, and the Prince Consort might order a prefabricated ballroom for Balmoral in 1851; but this did not prevent the English bishops from refusing to consecrate prefabricated churches in 1853. It seems paradoxical that, when a break was eventually made with the revivalist outlook of the nineteenth century, the first impulse came not from industry but from the Arts and Crafts Movement (which will be examined more closely in the chapter on the Precious Arts) whose adherents from 1861 onwards resisted collaboration with industry as far as they could. A parallel influence contributed to the development of the Catalan Antoni Gaudí i Cornet (1852–1926), the most phenomenal architect of his period.

As a student in Barcelona, Gaudí sat at the feet of Milá y Fontanals, whose lectures on aesthetics were coloured by his youthful association with the Nazarenes in Rome and his sympathy with the Pre-Raphaelites. Catalonian Nationalists at the time had a nostalgia for the Middle Ages which they identified with the golden age of their country. In this atmosphere Gaudí absorbed a respect for good craftsmanship, a liking for symbolism and a romantic feeling for nature; but he went further than any of his contemporaries in regarding natural forms as a source of inspiration for structure as well as for decoration. One of his earliest assignments was to assist the architects Villar and Fontseré in a project for adding a porch to the monastery church of Montserrat. In 1883 he took over the building of the proposed Expiatory Temple of the Holy Family in Barcelona, for which Villar had received the commission two years before. Gaudí completed the crypt by 1891 and the outer walls of the chevet by 1893 without substantially altering Villar's conventional Gothic design, although his mouldings and decorative details are less geometrical; but in the 'nineties a dramatic change occurred in his style which was almost in the nature of a conversion.

He made new plans which look like something seen in a vision. Henry-Russell Hitchcock in his book on nineteenth- and twentieth-century architecture (in *The Pelican History of Art*) says: "*In posse* the Sagrada Familia is perhaps the greatest ecclesiastical monument of the last hundred years. . . . However, Gaudí's church remains a fragment and a very incoherent one at that, even though he prepared in 1925, the year before his death, a brilliant new project for the nave." Work went on until 1914 and was resumed after the First World War, but only one façade of the transept has been completed. Craftsmen are still busy in a workshop on the site, but there is a hallucinatory quality about the whole scheme which makes one doubt if it will ever be realized.

The citizens of Barcelona, whatever their age, class or education, are almost unanimous in regarding the Sagrada Familia with admiration, pride and affection. To outsiders, however, the unfinished shell more often appears bizarre, vulgar or even ridiculous, though some find its upward surge inspiring. The city of Barcelona, trapped between mountains and sea, has an atmosphere of its own which is humid and oppressive. At night, the four slim tapering towers of the Sagrada Familia soar up to the sky like rockets; but in the heat of the day they remind one of great candles guttering in the sun. The carved stone of the façade seems to melt into shapeless heaps like wax; and yet, on closer inspection the structure is seen to be vertebrate enough and the sculpture is too closely integrated with it to be considered as mere ornament. The human figures are commonplace, but a whole world of organic forms reveals an imagination which anticipates the Surrealists. All Gaudí's motifs are derived from nature—bones, muscles, wings, plant-forms, clouds, caves and snowdrifts. Although his style could be described as basically Gothic with Art

Nouveau overtones, his interpretation is highly original and in many ways prophetic. His spaces look as though they have been hollowed out by erosion in a way that has since become familiar in the work of Henry Moore and Barbara Hepworth. The mosaic which decorates the pinnacles of the towers made use of broken glass and pottery long before the *objet trouvé* or Kurt Schwitter's *Merzbilder* became fashionable. The inspiration for these pinnacles came from native buildings which Gaudí had seen in Africa, and is of interest because, although primitive elements were widely borrowed in the painting and sculpture of the early twentieth century, they were rare in architecture. Gaudí first experimented with them in a project for a Franciscan mission in Tangier (1892–3) which was never carried out. In fact, most of his ecclesiastical designs remain unbuilt or unfinished, and his reputation rests more securely on his equally extraordinary secular work, which every *taxista* in Barcelona can point out to his passengers.

The unique aspect of his genius, in my opinion, is the rational basis that underlies all his buildings, however romantic and irrational they may appear. A good example may be found in the little church of the Colonia Güell outside Barcelona (1898–1914), which is only the crypt of a proposed church. It looks exactly like a folly erected in the park of an eccentric nobleman, and it was planned by means of a model resembling a cat's cradle. This model was made of string which represented the structural ribs of the building, and it was hung with weights proportional to the loads which each member would have to carry. In the words of Alexandre Cirici-Pellicer, author of *El arte modernista catalán*, "the polygons formed by these strings gave the inverted shape of the building's columns. It permitted a type of vaulted structure without buttresses of any kind, since all thrusts are taken up by suitably inclined pillars." This "funicular" principle was later adapted to the nave of the

Sagrada Familia. The Colonia Güell church might have been built for the inhabitants of Karel Čapek's insect kingdom. The columns lead inward as though the whole weight of the earth was pressing down on them: the window panes are shaped like moths' wings and have affinities with Lalique jewellery: the benches remind one of some curious insect. (More will be said about Gaudí's details and furnishings in the chapter on the Precious Arts.) Towards the end of his career he said: "The straight line belongs to man, the curved to God." The structural systems based on hyperboloids and paraboloids which was one of his last works has not yet been thoroughly studied.

Mention must be made in this short chapter of two important buildings which, although they cannot rival Gaudí's conceptions in originality, at least evince some degree of imagination and have the practical virtue of being structurally complete and in daily use. I refer to the basilica of the Sacred Heart in Paris and Westminster Cathedral in London.

The most interesting features of the Sacré Cœur are its magnificent situation on Montmartre and the circumstances in which it was built. The *Butte* on which it stands is a sandstone outcrop rising to about 400 feet to the north of Paris. It has been a venerated spot since pagan times. In antiquity it was crowned with a temple of Mercury, and in the Middle Ages with a shrine (now rebuilt) of St Denis, protomartyr of Paris. Nearby is the twelfth-century church of Saint-Pierre in which St Bernard, Dante and St Ignatius Loyala once prayed. In 1873, the National Assembly, by 393 votes to 164, decided to erect a national shrine there, and three million people throughout France subscribed to the building fund. The competition for its design was won by Paul Abadie (1812–84) and the building was finished by Lucien Magne (1849–1916). In the same year that he began to work on the Sacré Cœur, Abadie became diocesan architect of Périgueux, and it is rather difficult to decide how much his overenthusiastic restoration of the Romanesque cathedral of Saint-Front at Périgueux owed to his own design for the Sacré Cœur, and how much inspiration he found in the Romanesque building for the plans of the new basilica. The building of the Sacré Cœur presented serious technical difficulties. The soft sandstone of the *Butte* was riddled with quarries and wells, and the foundations had to be supported by concrete pillars sunk to the bedrock. Archeological though its design may be, it might well have been much worse, and in certain atmospheric conditions its cluster of white domes shimmers above Paris like a mirage, a tourist symbol as familiar as the Eiffel Tower and far more noble.

The site of Westminster Cathedral could scarcely be more different from that of the Sacré Cœur. Flat and hemmed in by other buildings, it affords no vantage point from which an impressive view of the cathedral can be seen. Far from being a hallowed spot, it has a history which can only be called chequered. It has been by turns a marsh reclaimed by the Benedictine monks of Westminster Abbey, a market and fairground, a maze, a pleasure-garden, a bull-baiting ring, an internment camp (after the battle of Worcester) and a prison. The land was bought by Cardinal Manning in 1884, but we have to thank Cardinal Vaughan for the fact that the cathedral is not, like Sir Giles Gilbert Scott's Anglican Cathedral at Liverpool (begun in 1904), yet another souvenir of the Gothic revival. The architect was not chosen by means of a competition. John Francis Bentley (1839–1902), a convert to Catholicism since 1862, was given the commission. He had originally trained as an engineer, but afterwards studied architecture under Henry Clutton, whose work has been considered in an earlier chapter. Bentley's previous output, which included St Mary's, Cadogan Street, London (1875–9), Corpus Christi, Brixton Hill, London (1886–7), Holy Rood, Watford (1887) and the Redemptorist monastery at Clapham (1891–3), had nearly all been Gothic in inspiration, and the first plan considered for the new metropolitan church was no exception. Cardinal Vaughan, however, sent Bentley off on an extensive tour to study Byzantine architecture. His interest in the style was not purely aesthetic. It was felt that a Gothic cathedral would appear to be competing with the nearby abbey, and a sufficiently large and dignified building in stone would cost far too much. A brick building would be much cheaper and the basic structure could be erected comparatively quickly: its embellishment could continue over a period of years as funds became available. The domed architecture of Byzantium with its early Christian traditions seemed to fulfil these requirements, besides offering the space needed for solemn ceremonies and large congregations.

Bentley made good use of the opportunities offered to him. Like the Sacré Cœur, Westminster Cathedral is much better than one might have expected a church of its period to be. The fabric was completed in 1903, only seven years after it was begun, but neither the founder nor the architect survived to see the building in use. Bentley died in 1902 and his patron a few months later: the Cardinal's requiem was the first public service held in the cathedral.

Reference is made to individual works of art at Westminster in the appropriate chapters. A list of some of the stones used in the interior reads like an old description of the Heavenly Jerusalem—jasper and opal and lapis lazuli, onyx and porphyry and pavonazzo, pentelic and cipollino and Carrara marble; but perhaps the nicest historic touch is lent by the verde antico columns in the nave, the "fresh green stone of Thessaly". The Larissa quarries, which are the only sources of this marble in the world, yielded material for Santa Sophia in the days of Justinian, but had been forgotten for centuries. On the way to England the columns were seized by the Turks, who were at war with Greece, and were delayed for several months.

The design of the cathedral is much better adapted to public participation in the liturgy than a Neo-Gothic building would have been. The nave, which is the widest in England, allows a seated congregation of 2,000 to see the sanctuary, and there is room for many more in the galleries and aisles. At the time of writing, provision has been made for Mass facing the people by the erection of an altar at the foot of the sanctuary steps, in the crossing of the transept. It has been fitted with a canopy which, instead of giving it more importance, is rather reminiscent of a stall in a bazaar; but this is obviously a temporary arrangement, and a better solution will no doubt be found.

CHAPTER VIII

BRIGHT PAVILIONS

We have already seen that although new materials and techniques had been adopted in the nineteenth century, ecclesiastical architects had not yet found a corresponding new language in which to express themselves. The general feeling seems to have been that it was all very well to experiment with the designs for multi-storey buildings in America, international exhibitions, department stores or private houses for rich eccentrics; but a church ought to have certain familiar adjuncts or it would not look like a church.

On the whole, the first years of the new century were less adventurous and inventive than the nineties, which had produced Art Nouveau and the best of the Chicago skyscrapers. Most of the Catholics in Westminster compared their new metropolitan church unfavourably with the Neo-Gothic cathedral which the twenty-two years old Giles Gilbert Scott had designed for the Anglicans of Liverpool, beating his own chief and 102 other rivals in the competition. Sir John Ninian Comper (1864–1960) talked about "eliminating time and producing an atmosphere of heavenly worship", an effect which he tried to achieve by building well-lit and spacious churches, usually in a Neo-Perpendicular style with a skilled blend of classical and other elements. He was much admired for his impeccable taste, and will be referred to again later, as his versatility and long life bring him to our notice more than once.

Art Nouveau, short-lived though it was and concerned

more with decoration than with structure, was significant because it was the first architectural style in our period which was not some kind of revival or attempt at reform. Its importance is in commercial and domestic architecture rather than in the building of churches, probably because it outraged traditionalists; and it rapidly became vulgarized before withering like the parasitic plant that it so much resembled. We have observed that Gaudí's work in Barcelona, although personal to its creator, incorporated many of the biological features of this style. The nearest approach to Art Nouveau church architecture in England was St Mary the Virgin, Great Warley, Essex (1904), by C. Harrison Townsend (1850–1928) who also built the Bishopsgate Institute, the Whitechapel Art Gallery and the Horniman Museum in London. The interior of St Mary's was decorated by Sir William Reynolds Stephens (1862–1943) and is more typical of its period than the simple exterior.

Even the most striking churches built between 1900 and the First World War tended to be more or less romantic variations on historic themes, though with an increased feeling for light and space.

In Scandinavia, dramatic effects were achieved by adapting the traditional styles or materials of local village churches to much larger buildings. This intentional flouting of scale and proportion produced an emotional impact similar to that of Mannerist distortions. The best known example is probably the Grundvig Church in Copenhagen by Peter Vilhelm Jansen Klint (1853–1930). Designed in 1913, but not completed until long after the First World War, its sheer organ-like façade with crow-stepped gables is familiar to every tourist in Denmark. In Sweden, the great wooden church at Kiruna was built by Gustaf Wickman (1858–1916), and the splendidly situated Hogalids Church (1916–23) in Stockholm was the work of Ivar Tengbom (b. 1878). The Masthugg Church (1910–14) in Goteborg by

Sigfrid Ericson (b. 1870) has a tower suitable for a town hall rising out of an ensemble which looks rural and almost domestic, with reminiscences of the American Shingle Style. More original was the Engelbrekt Church in Stockholm (1904–14) by Lars Israel Wahlmann (1870–1952). With its parabolic arches and tall slender tower, it was destined to exert a considerable influence.

In France, Victor Laloux (1856–1937), builder of the Gare d'Orsay in Paris, designed the basilica of Saint-Martin at Tours. This was a domed monument of Romanesque inspiration like Vaudremer's Saint-Pierre de Montrouge, built forty years earlier, but it was a much more pedestrian building.

In Austria, Otto Wagner (1841–1918), a former exponent of Art Nouveau, built St Leopold, the costly chapel of the Steinhof Asylum at Penzing outside Vienna. It was under construction from 1904 until 1907, and was a large domed church sumptuously decorated with mosaics by Rudolph Jettman, stained glass by Kolo Moser, and sculpture by Othmar Schimkowitz and Richard Luksch.

In England, Sir Edward Lutyens (1869–1944) was the most celebrated architect of this period. He was inventive enough within an eclectic framework, but his imagination was not of the theatrical order which we have noted in his Scandinavian contemporaries. His proportions were good and the workmanship in all his buildings very sound, but he never came to terms with the newer movements in twentieth-century architecture. His design for the Catholic cathedral at Liverpool, which was on the grandiose scale of his Government buildings at New Delhi, had to be abandoned owing to mounting costs when only the crypt had been completed. (The plan which replaced it will be referred to later.) His best church is probably St Jude's, Hampstead Garden Suburb, in which a bold silhouette and fine brickwork make amends for the combined use of vaguely seventeenth-century, high Renaissance and even Romanesque elements.

In the United States, Neo-Gothic churches were still being built by Ralph Adams Cram (1863–1942) and his former partner Bertram Grosvenor Goodhue (1867–1924), and in 1906 the firm of McKim, Mead and White gave a Byzantine flavour to Madison Avenue Presbyterian Church, New York. In California, Spanish Colonial styles were still popular with many architects including Irving Gill (1870–1936) whose first Church of Christ Scientist in San Diego (1904–7) has elliptical arches and ornamental ironwork; but the presence of China and Japan across the Pacific, no farther away than Europe, seems to have made itself felt at this time and Bernard Ralph Maybeck (1862–1957) invested his Christian Science Church in Berkeley, Cal., with oriental features. This highly eclectic building, dating from 1910, has very low-pitched wide-spreading gables, and window tracery which owes something to both Gothic and Art Nouveau.

None of the architects so far mentioned in this chapter could be called a pioneer of twentieth-century building, although Wagner was a precursor of the modern movement. Among the first generation of twentieth-century architects the most influential were probably an American, Frank Lloyd Wright (1867 or 9–1959), a German, Peter Behrens (1868–1940), an Austrian, Adolf Loos (1870–1933) and a Frenchman, Auguste Perret (1874–1954). Frank Lloyd Wright was not a respecter of the past. He sought to initiate a tradition, which he described as "organic architecture", and he liked to regard it as "Usonian" rather than American. Most of his long career was devoted to buildings, especially private houses, outside the scope of the present study, but his influence on younger architects was enormous, and he was responsible for at least one church which was a key monument in the early years of the century. This was the Unity Church in Oak Park, Ill., (1906) which was built entirely in concrete with a slab roof. The exterior has the massive appearance of a blockhouse or even an Egyptian tomb (though there is nothing archeological in the detail). All the decoration is integrated with the structure, and the interior is almost square.

Behrens was concerned primarily with industrial design and architecture. Unlike Morris and his circle, he accepted the inevitability of an industrialized society and evolved a severely functional style which has a kind of classic monumentality. He designed all manner of simple straightforward prototypes for mass-production—glassware, electrical equipment, shop fittings and packaging. Among his pupils were Walter Gropius, Mies van der Rohe and Le Corbusier, the leading architects of the next generation.

Adolf Loos was not a prolific builder but he was a great preacher. In the words of Robert Delevoy, "Loos believed that a work divested of ornament is symbolic of pure and lucid thought and a high degree of civilization; that good form must find its beauty in the degrees of usefulness it expresses, and in the indissoluble unity of its parts." This rather puritanical doctrine found many disciples among the church builders of the 'twenties and 'thirties.

It was left to Perret to design the building which is recognized as the real forerunner of the modern church. He left the Ecole des Beaux Arts without taking his final examination and joined the family building firm which had been among the pioneers of reinforced concrete construction. By the end of the First World War he had established himself as the leading practitioner in ferro-concrete, which he had used for blocks of flats, the Garage Ponthieu, the Théâtre des Champs Elysées and a number of warehouses and factories. "When Perret erected the church of Notre-Dame at Le Raincy . . .", says Henry-Russell Hitchcock, "concrete came of age as a building material."

Le Raincy was one of those projects, not unusual in the history of ecclesiastical patronage, in which lack of funds proved to be a source of inspiration. In 1918 the Abbé Nègre was faced with the task of building a new church on the eastern outskirts of Paris. During the war prices had soared, and it was because he found the estimates of the conventional church architects prohibitive that he approached Perret, thus earning for himself the distinction of having commissioned a landmark in twentieth-century architecture. Notre-Dame du Raincy is not a beautiful building, neither is the actual plan revolutionary, but it reflects a new integrity and a new conception of the purpose of a church. The shell vault does not rest on the walls but on very slender pillars which offer scarcely any visual obstruction. The walls are a separate pierced screen carried round the interior space and filled with coloured glass (which will be referred to in the appropriate chapter). Although the general form is that of a basilica with aisles and an apse, there is no real division of parts. The bays produced by the small vaults running crosswise over the aisles are so open that the impression is of a single uninterrupted auditorium. The sanctuary is raised above the level of the nave but the shallow flight of steps does not have the effect of cutting off the altar from the congregation. The exterior is less satisfactory, perhaps because Perret tried to give his tower a Gothic silhouette by attaching concrete colonnettes of different heights. They have no structural justification and are merely devices to increase the impression of verticality.

Notre-Dame du Raincy (1922–3) was the turning point after which forms which had already become familiar in civil buildings began to be accepted for ecclesiastical architecture, and the influence of the liturgical movement[1] began to make itself felt in the lay-out of churches. This did not mean that revivalist styles were completely abandoned, nor did it ensure that all churches which followed

[1] On the evolution, history and principles of the liturgical movement, see *The Liturgical Movement* in this series.

current fashions—Expressionism, Constructivism, Functionalism, "International Style" or Brutalism—were really modern in plan. On the contrary, most churches continued to be anachronistic because however many "contemporary" gimmicks they paraded, their plans were still based on medieval conceptions of worship. Perret's second church, Sainte-Thérèse at Montmagny (Seine-et-Oise), built in 1925–6, was less successful than his first. It was nearly thirty years before he received another important ecclesiastical commission. This was for Saint-Joseph at Le Havre, a powerful, ugly giant which he did not live to see completed by Raymond Audigier in 1955.

The influence of Le Raincy is clearly seen in the churches of the 'twenties and 'thirties, among which St Antony at Basle deserves special mention. Built in 1926–7 by Karl Moser (1890–1936) this was the first important modern church in Switzerland. It looks rather like a bus station, but it is a very honest building in which the exterior is more in harmony with the interior than in Perret's prototype. The tower, which has often been imitated, is simpler and more satisfactory. Karl Moser taught the next generation of Swiss architects while professor at Zurich Technical College from 1915 to 1918.

It was in Germany that theologians and architects first began to co-operate in the design of churches based on changing liturgical ideals. Prominent in this movement was Rudolf Schwartz (1897–1961) whose church of Corpus Christi at Aachen (1928) is a single integrated space without pillars or enclosed sanctuary.[2] Another father of modern church architecture in Germany was Dominikus Böhm

[2] Schwartz had a philosophical approach to architecture which he expressed in his book *Vom Bau der Kirche* (1938), It was translated into English twenty years later as *The Church Incarnate*. His churches have something of the transcendent quality of Romanesque building, for he aimed at "inwardness" and did not like too many windows in his heavy walls.

(1880–1955), whose work in the 'twenties was more Expressionist in feeling and achieved dramatic effects with parabolic arches. His church of St Engelbert at Riehl (1931–3) was based on a circular plan and roofed not with a dome but with lobes of paraboloid barrel vaulting. Of these four churches—Notre-Dame at Le Raincy, St Antony at Basle, Corpus Christi at Aachen and St Engelbert at Riehl—Anton Henz has said: "All that has been built in succeeding decades and is now gaining ground in Europe and America as the ecclesiastical architecture of our day, has developed upon (their) foundations."

Whereas the commissions of Schwartz and Böhm were invariably Catholic, Otto Bartning (1883–1959) concentrated on Protestant churches. His steel church in Cologne (1928) and his circular church of the Resurrection at Essen were notable buildings of their period. Martin Weber built an octagonal church at Frankfurt-on-Main in 1926.

Architects elsewhere were beginning to break away from the more conventional rectangular type of plan. In Czechoslovakia, Professor A. Gocar built a trapezoidal church at Hradec Krălově in 1929. Even in England, unreceptive though it was to new ideas, two churches were built with central altars in the 1930's. The first was at Bradford, where J. H. Langtry Langton built the church of the First Martyrs to the requirements of Mgr John O'Connor, who wanted a building expressive of the corporate nature of Christian worship. When Eric Gill saw it he was so enthusiastic about the circular plan that he designed another church himself, cruciform but with a central altar, at Gorleston-on-Sea, Norfolk. Neither of these churches was outstanding architecturally, but they represented the earliest attempts at liturgical planning in this country. In the Church of England, John Keble Church, Mill Hill, London (consecrated 1937) was the first parish church to establish a closer relationship between clergy and people; and F. Cachemaille-Day's

St Michael and All Angels at Wythenshawe, Manchester (consecrated in 1937) was built on a star-shaped plan. Reinforced concrete was used in both of these buildings.

Although the international leaders of the generation following Wright, Behrens, Loos and Perret had reached maturity, they rarely at this period received commissions for churches; nevertheless, the influence of Walter Gropius (born 1883), Ludwig Mies van der Rohe (born 1886) and Charles-Edouard Jeanneret, known as Le Corbusier (1887–1965) was making itself felt in all branches of architecture. All three men communicated their ideas by teaching or writing as well as through their buildings.

In 1919 Gropius had been appointed director of both the Art School and the School of Arts and Crafts at Weimar. He combined them into a school of design, building and crafts, under the name of Das Staatliche Bauhaus, and carried out there a programme not unlike that of the English Arts and Crafts Movement in the 1880's, except that his attitude towards industry was more realistic. He advocated team work in building, and believed that the distinction between artists and craftsman should be eliminated. He also said: "It is essential to walk round a building in order to grasp its shape and the functions of its parts." From the 1920's this attitude gained ground, and architects began to design buildings intended to be viewed from any angle, with no part demanding prior attention. Many famous artists including Feininger, Kandinsky and Klee taught at the Bauhaus, which was closed by the National Socialists in 1933. By that time Mies van der Rohe had become director on the recommendation of Gropius, but conditions in Germany had become impossible for adherents of the modern movement, and there was an exodus of nearly all the leading architects. In addition to Gropius and Mies, Ludwig Hilbersheimer (born 1885), Marcel Breuer (born 1902), Martin Wagner (1885–1957), Erich Mendelsohn (1887–1953) and Hannes

Meyer (1889–1954) all emigrated, most of them across the Atlantic, where they shared with Frank Lloyd Wright the credit for injecting new life into American architecture. Mies is an architect of great integrity, classical in his principles, sometimes over austere but always to be admired for his craftsmanship. As director of the Illinois Institute of Technology at Chicago (for which he provided new buildings, including a chapel) he influenced a whole school of younger architects, more by example than by precept for he is less of a teacher than Gropius and less of a theorist than Le Corbusier. Le Corbusier's creative vision in which, as Maurice Besset has said, "Logic and lyric become one" will be discussed in connection with the 1950's.

One could scarcely expect the 1930's to be a brilliant period in the history of architecture. In addition to the rise of the Nazi party, the decade was haunted by international economic depression and the Spanish Civil War. In Italy the opposition between academic and "rationalist" groups, each claiming to serve the cause of Fascism, ended in confusion. As Giulia Veronesi has observed, "For two centuries now, Italian architects when they have not built like ancient Romans, have trodden in the steps of foreigners." It was tragic that the only men who might have restored Italy to a leading position in international architecture were victims of two world wars—Antonio Sant'Elia was killed at the age of thirty-six in 1916, and Giuseppe Terragni was only thirty-eight when he died in 1942 from the effects of his service on the Russian and Greek fronts.

One important project—Notre-Dame de Toutes Grâces at Assy—was initiated in France just before the outbreak of the Second World War but it was not completed until 1950, and as its significance lies less in its architecture than in the individual works of art which it contains, it will be included in the chapter on the Precious Arts. Notre-Dame de Toutes Grâces is typical of modern French churches in the sense that French artists have probably made a greater contribution to liturgical art than any in the world, but new French churches are on the whole structurally inferior to those in Germany and Switzerland.

In Holland, church building tended to be dominated by historicism and a romantic attitude towards craft work: when a leading architect such as Jacobus Johannes Pieter Oud (1890–1961) built an uncompromisingly modern church (for the Kiefhoek housing estate, Rotterdam, 1928–30), it was completely lacking in religious atmosphere.

Finland readily accepted new ideas in architecture and could claim in Hugo Henrik Alvar Aalto (b. 1898) a figure who commanded international respect. Eliel Saarinen (1873–1950) a founding father of Finnish modern building, had settled permanently in the United States in 1923.

It was Sweden, a latecomer to industrialism, that set the pace for Europe in the 1930's, though more in the fields of town planning and housing than in ecclesiastical architecture. The leading figures were Osvald Almquist (1884–1950), Gunnar Asplund (1885–1940) and Sigurd Lewerentz (b. 1885), all of the same age-group as Gropius, Mies and Le Corbusier. During the war, building did not come to a standstill in neutral Sweden as it did in most combatant countries, but isolation and shortage of supplies led to a reliance on local materials and a certain provincialism which continued until the 1950's.

Church building since the end of the Second World War has been on such a vast scale that Raoul Glaber's famous phrase about Europe throwing off her rags and tatters to don a "white mantle of churches" might have been written about our own time instead of the millennium. The scale of this building campaign is indicated by the fact that in a single city—Cologne—nearly fifty new churches have risen out of the rubble and ashes, and in a single country—France —the Catholic community alone has built more than 650 new places of worship. Such a subject could only be covered adequately in a large book, so I shall restrict myself to a general summary of characteristics and trends, pinpointing only the most outstanding architects and buildings. Two striking developments are immediately evident. The first is a much wider recognition than in the 'twenties and 'thirties of the need for new plans adapted to changing patterns of worship. The second is the final surrender—if only for reasons of economy—of ecclesiastical architects and their patrons to modern materials and techniques.

The traditional aisled basilica and hall-church have almost completely given way to plans designed to bring the congregation into closer touch with the altar, which instead of being a sort of sideboard pushed up against a wall has become a free-standing table or block of stone. Circular churches (of which a recent example is Sep Ruff's St John Capistran, Munich, 1960) are, of course, no novelty, for they were not uncommon in early Christian, Carolingian and Romanesque times; but there seems no limit to the variety of plans. Some are oval (Joseph Lehmbrock's St Albertus Magnus, Leverkusen-Sclebusch, 1959), ovoid with the altar in the narrow end (Gottfried Böhm's St Albert, Saarbrücken, 1958), or elliptical (Pierre Vago's enormous underground basilica of St Pius X, Lourdes, 1958): others are fan-shaped (Kaija and Haikki Siren's village church, Orivesi, Finland, 1961), paraboloid (Rudolf Schwartz's Holy Cross, Bottrop, 1957), or triangular (Arno Ruusuvuori's village church at Hyvinkää, Finland, 1961). Our Lady of the Angels, Vitoria (1959) by Javier Carvajal Ferrer and Garcia de Paredes, is sagittate, Josef Lackner's St Pius X, Innsbruck (1960) is square, and Rudolf Schwartz's St Anna, Düren, (1956) is L-shaped. Where the old rectangular form is retained, the altar may be placed parallel with one of the long walls (as in St Nicolas, Venlo, Limburg, by G. J. van der Grinten, 1961); or off-centre of a short wall (as in the Reformed Church,

Nagele, Noordoostpolder, by van den Broek and Bakema, 1960). Some churches are too unusual or complex for such a brief description and will be mentioned individually. It is no longer considered essential to have the main entrance on the altar axis.

Many churches, especially in Scandinavia, are divided into two or more unequal areas by sliding doors, so that small, medium and large congregations can be accommodated: in such cases the altar may be designed so that it can be used from two sides. A notable example is Alvar Aalto's Vuoksenniska Church, Imatra, Finland (1958) which has motor-driven doors capable of providing three areas for simultaneous use; others include Lewerentz's Markus Church, Stockholm-Björkhagen (1960), and Graae and Wohlert's Stengård Church, Copenhagen-Gladsaxe (1963). There is an increasing tendency to make the church one of a group of related buildings. The church of St Thomas (Peter Celsing, 1960) in the new development area of Vällingby, Stockholm, has a youth centre, parish hall, club-room, kitchen and cloak-rooms as well as the usual Swedish registry. Cloakrooms are almost a necessity in cold climates, where (for example) a bride might have to change into her wedding dress on arrival, after a cross-country journey through the snow. But it is not only in Scandinavia that we find this sort of ensemble: the church of Maria in den Benden (Düsseldorf-Wersten, 1959) by Emil Steffan and his associate Nicolaus Rosiny, has a kindergarten, office, and quarters for both priest and sacristan: and St Justina (in the new settlement of Santa Giustina near Mesola in the Po delta), built by Pierluigi Giordani in 1952, not only has a kindergarten, elementary school and community hall, but also an infirmary and a co-operative store grouped near it.

On the whole, the finest and most liturgical buildings are in Germany, Switzerland and Eastern France. With certain exceptions, it can be said that the farther one goes from the sources of the liturgical movement, the more architects cling to out-dated plans. Sir Basil Spence has made imaginative use of contemporary artists and has added superficially modern touches to his romantic cathedral at Coventry, (1954–62) but its plan is no more geared to present-day needs than Sir Edward Maufe's more frankly traditional cathedral at Guildford (designed in 1936). Robert Maguire's church at Bow Common, London (1960) is a more successful attempt to provide a liturgical plan for Anglican worship. Many of the new churches in Sweden are beautiful buildings, but their elongated dressed-up altars cling obstinately to the east wall of a rectangular plan.

There is a widespread feeling that churches ought not to be entered too abruptly, but should be designed with a "preparation space" in the form of a courtyard, garden, cloister or at least a well-defined narthex. There could be two schools of thought about this. There is some justification for thinking that the church should be part and parcel of our daily lives, not something set apart. It is, however, a good idea to have a place where parishioners can congregate and become acquainted after services. Among the churches which provide pleasant enclosures of this kind are St Mauritius, Saarbrücken, with fountain court and cloister (architect Albert Dietz, associate Bernard Grothe, 1958): the Paul Gerhardt Church, Mannheim, with enclosed parvis and fountain (Gerhardt Schlegel and Reinhold Kergil, 1961): St John Capistran, Munich, with garden entrance: the Markus Church, Stockholm-Björkhagen, with pool and trees: and the Baranzate Church, Milan (Mangiarotti and Morassutti, 1958) with a garden parvis that seems to have exceeded its limits, for the church too is full of potted plants.

Apart from changes aiming at a closer relationship between priest and congregation, some thought has been given to the position and design of pulpits and fonts. Improved acoustics and the movement away from long naves have combined to abolish the need for lofty pulpits with sounding-boards, set well forward among the congregation. In Catholic churches the tendency is towards an ambo (or ambos) in or near the sanctuary (as in St Anna, Düren, and Hans Schädel's St Joseph, Hasloch-am-Main, 1958). These may have some decorative link with the altar. The Pontifical rules that "he who reads the Word of God shall be in an elevated position, easily visible". In Nonconformist and Reformed churches the pulpit has always been given great prominence, and today the communion table, font and pulpit are sometimes placed in close proximity, sharing equal importance.

The position of the baptistery is rather a problem, because it should be accessible from the exterior as well as from the church. According to the American directives it is to be "located near the entrance of the church. The holy font should make a strong statement to the community entering for divine worship." The dignity of the sacrament of baptism demands that the font should not be poked away in a corner, and the new Paschal regulations decree that the ceremonies at the font should be performed before the whole congregation. The position in the sanctuary (sometimes, as we have seen, adopted in Reformed churches) is obviously not in accord with Catholic liturgy, and perhaps the best solution might be to have a spacious narthex incorporating the baptistery, especially if a glass partition or sliding doors allowed an unobstructed view from the nave. There is a great diversity of practice. The usual arrangement is to have the baptistery divided off near the entrance, but sometimes the font is not enclosed (as in Schwartz's St Michael, Frankfurt-am-Main, 1954, where it is in line with the altar). Dominikus Böhm's Maria Königin, Cologne (1954) has a separate circular baptistery, accessible without entering the church and connected with the main building by a glazed passage at the altar end. Guillaume Gillet's Notre-Dame at

Royan, Charente Maritime (1958), has its baptistery (also accessible from the exterior at the altar end) marked by a small tower. The Protestant Church of St Thomas, Väl-lingby, has an enormous font more than two yards square, with constantly running water. St Boniface, Dortmund, has a curious baptistery designed by Emil Steffann and H. G. Bücker, in which a circular sunken font surrounded by iron railings has its cover raised by a sort of pulley attached to the ceiling, from which is suspended the figure of a dove.

When we come to consider new building materials and methods we find that for the first time these are being accepted honestly and without self-consciousness. On the one hand, most architects have freed themselves from the nineteenth-century practice of using modern means to express revivalist forms, while on the other hand they have moved away from the austere viewpoint of the 1920's which was summed up by Bruno Taut when he said: "Serviceability becomes the actual context of aesthetics." Even sentiment has crept back, as we can see from the decision taken by so many architects to retain the surviving towers of bombed buildings, regardless of their artistic merit: Spence at Coventry, Egon Eiermann in the Kaiser Wilhelm Memorial Church, Berlin, Dieter Oesterlan in Christ Church, Bochem and St Martin's, Hanover, and Paul Schneider-Esleben in St Rochus, Düsseldorf, are only a few examples.

Reinforced concrete provides the structural framework of most churches, but traditional materials are still favoured where they are readily available and economically feasible. It seems obvious that Rudolf Schwartz preferred to use local stone and bricks wherever possible, and Swedish churches are notable for their fine brickwork. The village church of Gravberget, Norway (the last work of Magnus Poullson, 1956), is built entirely of wood with imbricated shingles like the medieval *stavkirken*, and the interior is full of folksy paintings. Timber lines the soaring vaults of most tent-roofed churches, and laminated wood is widely employed, especially in America. For floors, wood, brick, tiles or stone are more often chosen than concrete; marble and terrazzo are still used, particularly in Italy and Spain, and slate is deservedly popular in France and Germany. Copper roofs and decorative elements are found in some churches such as Carl Nyren's Västetort Church, Stockholm-Vällingby (1956) and Ernst Gisel's Reformed Church, Effretikon, Switzerland (1961). Among the less conventional materials one might single out the asbestos roof and upper exterior walls of the Technical University Chapel, Otaniemi, Helsinki (Kaija and Heikki Siren, 1957). The walls of the Baranzate Church, Milan-Vialba, are composed of inch-thick foam plastic between two layers of glass. This has an insulating effect and keeps the church cool in the hottest weather. Being translucent, it also admits a soft diffused light, but the plastic has worn badly and in the course of seven years has become streaked and discoloured. Clear acrylic plastic is used instead of glass for the oculus which concentrates light on the sanctuary in St John Capistran, Munich.

Where new techniques such as suspended roofs, space frames and shell structures are involved, the architect often collaborates with an engineer. This was the case in Notre-Dame de Royan, which incorporates several structural developments pioneered by its engineer Bernard Lafaille. The thin saddle roof which defies the Atlantic gales is only one of its interesting technical features. Eugène Freyssinet was responsible for solving the engineering problems of the underground basilica of St Pius X at Lourdes, from which 22,000 people can be evacuated in fifteen minutes. The roof of St Albert, Saarbrücken, is hung by steel cables, and that of St John Capistran, Munich, extends outside to form a covered way supported by weighted columns. The church of the Most Holy Redeemer, Turin-Mirafiori (by a father and son partnership, Nicola and Leonardo Mosso, 1957) has a fantastic vault engineered by Livio Norzi, which admits slanting rays of light through a series of roof-slits. Effective means have been found everywhere to prevent glare, by allowing light to enter from sources unseen by the congregation when they are facing the altar, as in Coventry Cathedral, Miguel Fisac's church of the Coronation of Our Lady, Vitoria, Spain (1960), the Madonna of the Poor, Milan, by Luigi Fegini and Gino Pollini (1952), and Dieter Oesterlan's Christ Church, Bochem (1959). External noise from busy thoroughfares has been excluded by means of double walls, as in the Kaiser Wilhelm Memorial Church, Berlin, where the five-foot space between the inner and outer glass walls accommodates the artificial lighting, also visible from the exterior. Acoustics have been improved with the aid of a cork ceiling in Madrid's Theological Seminary Chapel (José Luis Fernández de Amo, 1962), and a sanctuary wall and ceiling which curve forward in Alvar Aalto's Vuoksenniska Church, Imatra, Finland.

There are a number of systems involving the spatial dissolution of stresses, often by means of light steel grids. Space-frame roof-trusses are often left exposed as in the Paul Gerhardt Church, Mannheim, Joachim Schürmann's St Pius, Cologne-Flittard (1961), Hentrich and Petschnigg's Christ Church, Leverkusen-Bürig, and Our Lady of the Angels, Vitoria, where they make an airy network which to a woman is rather reminiscent of a rack for airing laundry.

Shell structures are those in which a thin curved material resistant to tension and compression is used instead of beam-type support structure. The principle exists in nature where the strength of an egg or snail-shell is out of all proportion to its thickness. Although their practical advantages were first demonstrated in Germany by Walter Bauersfeld and Franz Dischinger, shell structures seem to have been used in a particularly adventurous and imaginative way by Latin architects and engineers, such as Pier Luigi Nervi (b. 1891) and Eduardo Torroja (1899–1961) who have spanned vast areas with shells only an inch or two in thickness. Torroja designed the first really modern churches to be built in the Iberian Peninsula, including one at Xerallo (the Ascension, 1952) which is a fantasia on a series of egg-shapes. He had a decisive influence on a younger Spanish architect, Felix Candela (b. 1910) who left Spain to settle in Mexico in 1939. This brings us to one of the most fascinating developments in modern architecture—the new buildings which have blossomed like tropical flowers in Central and South America.

Mexico was the first of the Latin-American countries to evolve an autochthonous modern architecture, at first strictly functional but later allowing more scope (sometimes too much) to the traditional love of decoration. Its pioneer was José Villagrán Garcia (b. 1901) but its greatest contribution to twentieth-century building has been Candela's development of shell construction. Henry-Russell Hitchcock says that he "works with ferro-concrete vaults . . . with the casual ease and *ad hoc* ingenuity of a twelfth-century Frenchman building in stone". The influence of Gaudí can be recognized in his church of the Miraculous Virgin in Mexico City (1953–5). He collaborated with Enrique de la Mora y Palomar (b. 1907) for the Chapel of the Holy Ghost Missionaries, Coyoacán (1956); and de la Mora himself built the striking church of the Most Pure Virgin at Monterrey, Mexico (1939–47). Colombia and Venezuela have since joined Mexico in erecting buildings which challenge any in Europe; and even Puerto Rico has an impressive church (St Martin de Porres at Cataño outside San Juan) built by Henry Klumb (b. 1905) a pupil of Frank Lloyd Wright.

The most spectacular achievements in South America, however, have been in Brazil, where a good tradition of local Baroque had existed before the importation of dull academic French styles in the early nineteenth century. The new architecture retains certain colonial features such as jalousies, ceramic tiles and mosaic, and uses modern methods and materials in its own daring, dramatic way. Brazilian architects have been profoundly influenced by Le Corbusier who in 1936 spent a few weeks in Rio de Janeiro as consultant for the Ministry of Education project. His lyrical approach and his favourite concepts of *pilotis* and *brises soleil* were equally suited to the national temperament and to the climate. The doyen of Brazilian architects is Lúcio Costa (b. 1902), who was the first to notice and sponsor the bold inventive talents of Oscar Niemeyer Soares Filho (b. 1907), now regarded as the leading figure in Brazilian architecture. Niemeyer was given the colossal task of designing all the main public buildings in Brasilia, the new capital (1956–61). His cathedral there has influenced Frederick Gibberd's circular plan for the Catholic cathedral now in process of construction at Liverpool, but his most famous church is that of St Francis at Pampulha (1943). This almost Baroque style with its sweeping curves and general air of exuberance has been imitated by many Latin-American architects who lack Niemeyer's assurance and taste. Examples are Juvenal Moya's Our Lady of Fatima (1953–4) and the Chapel of the Ginnasio Moderno (1954–5), both in Bogota, Colombia.

It is hardly surprising to find that places of worship in North America, especially those serving Protestant communities, are usually more sober in design, such as Pietro Belluschi's First Presbyterian Church, Oregon (1951). Elial Saarinen (1873–1950) who was the leading Finnish architect before he settled in the United States in 1923, designed a series of churches and chapels of which the best-known are the Tabernacle Church, Columbus, Ind. (1940–2) and the similar but smaller Christ Lutheran Church, Minneapolis (1948–50). He was noted for his handsome brickwork and his effective management of space. He formed a partnership with his son Eero (1910–61) who built the circular red brick chapel at the Massachusetts Institute of Technology (1954–5). In the latter part of his career Frank Lloyd Wright designed a number of churches including the Pfeiffer Chapel, Florida Southern College, Lakeland, Florida (1948), the First Unitarian Church, Madison, Wis. (1961), a Greek Orthodox Church (his wife's faith) for Milwaukee, Wis. (1961) and the Pilgrim Congregational Church, Redding, Cal., built since his death. For the Catholic community some respectable churches have been built by Barry Byrne (St Columba in St Paul, Minnesota, St Francis Xavier in Kansas City) and Paul Thirsy, Fox and Ballas (St Anthony in Massoula, Montana); but by far the most important project has been that undertaken by Marcel Breuer for St John's Abbey, Collegeville, Minnesota.

Breuer (b. 1902 in Hungary) had been one of the youngest pupils of Gropius at the Bauhaus. After emigrating to the United States he acted as associate professor at Harvard under Gropius, who also took him into partnership. He has a distinguished reputation as a teacher but is sometimes criticized for giving equal importance to each part of his buildings thereby detracting from their effect as a group. In 1953 he was commissioned to prepare a master plan for monastic buildings which may not be finished for a century. The first items scheduled for completion were the church, monastic wing, students' dormitory and library. Breuer says that although the church may be a new sensation to the eye, its architectural concepts are in some ways traditional. It is shaped by the liturgy. The plan is in the form of a bell with choir stalls surrounding the sanctuary in the wider end. Side walls and roof are a series of concrete folds, which contain most of the equipment for lighting and ventilation and also have acoustic functions. The north façade is a window wall with separate hexagonal panes set in a concrete grille. A free-standing concrete slab forming a "bell-banner" stands astride the entrance, acting as a gateway as well as a modern version of the traditional campanile. Abbot Baldwin declared at the outset that "the Benedictine tradition at its best challenges us to think boldly and to cast our ideals in forms which will be valid for years to come, shaping them with all the genius of present-day materials and techniques". The church was finished in 1961.

In the long history of architecture, few small buildings have created such a stir as Le Corbusier's pilgrimage chapel of Notre-Dame du Haut, Ronchamp, Haute-Saône (1950-5). It has excited extremes of opinion. Frank Lloyd Wright dismissed Le Corbusier as "only a painter and not a very good one". G. E. Kidder Smith has said: "It is doubtful if a finer church has been built since Brunelleschi's 1446 Pazzi Chapel . . . it is the greatest building of our time." The majority view is highly favourable. Although it is liturgically workmanlike, it is an extremely romantic conception. Le Corbusier studied the site and allowed himself to be influenced by the landscape and the line of the horizon. He said that the curious roof was inspired by the shell of a crab, but most people see it as the prow of a ship and to me it suggests —perhaps because of its brown and white colour scheme— some strange new kind of mushroom growing naturally out of the hilltop. It is a perfect exemplar of the Gropius theory that no building should have an ideal viewpoint. Ronchamp demands to be seen from every angle, or rather from every curve. One of the reasons for its appeal is its primitive quality. From the exterior, the south wall with its apparently random fenestration reminds one of a cliff riddled with cave openings; inside, the ceiling sags like the canopy of a tent and the only artificial light is provided by votive candles. After ten years the rough concrete looks rather shabby, but the strange shape has lost none of its magic. It has had an enormous influence, both in the general sense of having released a more emotional approach on the part of other architects, and in the specific sense of having been widely imitated in its details. Soaring tent roofs such as those recently built at St Cloud and Marly-le-Roi are examples of the general romantic influence, and individual features (such as the deepset unsymmetrical windows or the upswept roof resting not on the walls but on supports which allow a strip of light to enter) have been reflected in dozens of churches from Hans Schilling's St Alban in Cologne to Gresleri's Church of the Immaculate Conception at Bologna, and from Karel Sijmon's Dutch Reformed Church at Aerdenhout to Hermann Baur's Brüderklausen Church at Birsfelden in Switzerland.

Although Le Corbusier was responsible for a great many important undertakings such as his *Unités d'Habitation* and the public buildings in Chandigarh, his only other ecclesiastical work was the Dominican priory of La Tourette, Eveux-sur-l'Arbresle near Lyons (1957–60). Its chapel is indirectly lit by odd cylindrical elements like ship's funnels or huge gun-barrels (Le Corbusier called them *canons à lumière*) pointing in different directions to trap the sun at all hours of the day. Each admits a different coloured light.

It is, I think, true to say that Le Corbusier with these two buildings and Rudolf Schwartz with his much more extensive œuvre have made the most important individual contributions to modern church architecture. It is interesting to compare their very different achievements. Schwartz produced a steady stream of churches such as St Michael, Frankfurt-on-Main (1954), St Anna, Düren (1956), Holy Cross, Bottrop (1957) and Maria Königin, Saarbrücken (1959), all maintaining a high level of excellence. They are substantial, reassuring, and carefully worked out for Catholic worship by a Catholic whose mind was given to philosophy and metaphysics. They are usually fortresslike without and (in their designer's own words) "mighty refuges" within. They are well finished and built to last for centuries. There is nothing light-hearted about them although they are airy and well-lit. Le Corbusier on the other hand was untypical of his Swiss Calvinist background in being lyrical and sketchy. There is some truth in the accusation that his values were sculptural rather than architectonic; but there is method in what Maurice Besset has called his apparent wilfulness. His sense of proportion was unerring and his modular system, which relates the scale of his buildings with that of a man's body, has helped to restore humanity to architecture. The rather shoddy finish that often detracts from the quality of his work may be seen as an outward expression of his own valuation of himself: his buildings are blueprints for the future rather than monuments for posterity.

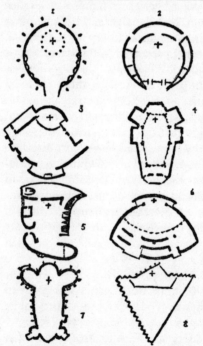

1. St Albert, Saarbrücken, 1957 (Gottfried Böhm)

2. St John Capistran, Munich, 1960 (Sep Ruf)

3. Bruder Klausen Church, Birsfalden, Switzerland, 1959 (Herman Baur)

4. Santa Maria Maggiore, Francavilla - al - Mare, 1959 (Ludovico Quavoni)

5. Notre Dame du Haut, Ronchamp, 1955 (Le Corbusier)

6. Village Church, Orivesi, Finland, 1961 (Kaija & Heikki Siren)

7. St Michael, Frankfurt, 1954 (Rudolf Schwartz)

8. Village Church, Hyrinkää, 1961 (Aarno Ruusuvuori)

Alternatives to the rectangular plan for churches. Sketch plans not drawn to scale.

CHAPTER IX

THE PRECIOUS ARTS

It is customary for art historians, after devoting considerable space to architecture, painting and sculpture, to end with a summary survey of the so-called "minor" or "applied" arts. These inept and condescending terms are used to describe some of the world's greatest masterpieces—faïences from Pharaonic Egypt, the chariot mascot from Ur of the Chaldees, seals and coins from ancient Athens and Syracuse, the Imperial cameo of Vienna, the Tassilo chalice, the Lewis chessmen, and the Syon cope. For reasons of convenience, I too have been obliged to crowd into one chapter metalwork, stained glass, mosaics, ceramics and textiles; but I have chosen to call them the precious arts for, apart from the intrinsic value of the materials, the degree of rather mysterious skill involved has always made them costly, sought after and jealously treasured. The earliest "status symbols" were metalwork, leather and textiles, and even today, races like the Arabs who have a nomadic history prefer to count their wealth in portable possessions such as fine weapons and carpets.

WORK IN PRECIOUS METALS

In primitive societies the smith, in his capacity of armourer, was held in the highest esteem and regarded as something of a magician. It was thought that he owed his artistry to divinities whom the Greeks identified under such names as Corybantes, Dactyls, Telchines and Cyclopes. In Homeric times the smith himself became a god, but the name by which we know him—Hephaistos—is older than the Greek language. Just as the myth of Homer's blindness arose because minstrelsy was a calling which a blind man could follow, the myth of the Olympian smith's lameness probably arose because a smith needed strong arms rather than strong legs. Because he commanded so much respect he was often the chief counsellor of the king or tribal chief, and this tradition survived into Christian times as we know from the legends of Saint-Eloi and St Dunstan.

I propose to use the term "goldsmith" to include the silversmith, for the tools and techniques used by both are identical. Goldsmiths' work, which sometimes incorporates enamelling and jewellery and from very early times has also been associated with ivory carving, is one of the great glories of Christian art: so splendid were its past achievements that the ecclesiastical goldsmiths of the late eighteenth and early nineteenth centuries were content to base their work on the patterns of earlier times. In the Church of England, some altar plate was still made in the sober and dignified style of the Commonwealth, but most Catholic churches naturally favoured Renaissance or Baroque models. Stonyhurst owns a chalice (mark of William Pitts and Joseph Preedy, 1791) which has the tall baluster-like form and small cup which we recognize as Spanish in origin, and there is a later example in Westminster Cathedral treasury (mark of Robert Hennell, 1830) which is not dissimilar. Other interesting survivals from this period are a censer like a sugar sifter with chains (mark of Charles Kandler, 1786) at Wardour Castle, an Adam-inspired sanctuary lamp of 1789 at Arundel Castle, and a monstrance of 1808 at Stonyhurst (mark of Samuel Hennell) which has an over-sized crown on the top and curious little lambrequins draped over the rays.

With the Gothic revival there was, of course, a return to medieval types, and Pugin and other architects designed

church plate of the "correct" kind. Individual craftsmen
usually worked for church furnishers such as John Hardman
or Skidmore's Art Manufacturing Company. Hardman's,
established in 1838, began as a small shop in Birmingham
with a modest trade in such *dix-huitième* necessities as snuff-
boxes and shoe-buckles. A meeting between Pugin and John
Hardman's son led to the establishment of a workshop for
carrying out Pugin's designs in metal and glass. The firm's
reputation was made by the Great Exhibition in 1851, at
which their only serious rivals were the French partnership of
Poussielgue et Rusand. Hardman's products can be seen in
cathedrals, colleges and churches all over the British Empire
and the United States. Viollet-le-Duc designed *orfèvrerie*
which was executed by Poussielgue et Rusand. At the Paris
Exhibition of 1855, the *Ecclesiologist* had to admit that
French goldsmiths' work was much finer in execution than
English, and far superior in its handling of enamel and
precious stones; but it was not considered so "correct" from
an archeological point of view. This revivalist outlook survived almost until the end of the century, although a few of
the more original designers such as William Burges and
J. D. Sedding added individual touches of their own.

In Spain, Gaudí designed altar plate and church furnishings as unique and extraordinary as his architecture. In the
treasury of Tarragona Cathedral there is a monstrance in his
style, though not actually made by him, which has a fairytale
beauty of pale gilt and pale jewels more suited to Aladdin's
cave than to a place on the altar. His ironwork was particularly striking. He used it in great profusion on his buildings,
where it writhes and cavorts like a live creature, and he
designed everything down to locks and bolts. One of the most
interesting aspects of Gaudí's wayward genius is that the
dreams on his drawing-board, fantastic though they seemed,
actually worked. His odd-looking benches in the little
Church of the Colonia Güell near Barcelona are in fact

completely functional. If one may distort a phrase of Le Corbusier's, they are perfect machines for sitting or kneeling on, and they also allow one to stand up, which is more than can be said of most church seating.

The architect J. D. Sedding had a pupil, later his chief assistant, called Henry Wilson (1864–1934). During Sedding's lifetime, the pupil's work was often indistinguishable from that of the master; but from 1891, after Sedding's death, Wilson taught metalwork at the Royal College of Art where he became entangled in the luxuriant vegetation of Art Nouveau. The chalice which he made for the church of St Bartholomew, Brighton, is one of the most extraordinary manifestations of this style. With an amorphous lump of blue and green enamel for a knop, elaborate carved ivory decoration, intricate chasing and an inscription which reminds one of the lettering on the Paris Métro, it is a remarkable and vigorous feat of craftsmanship in which one can almost hear the sap rising. It is quite hideous and most impractical. Also influenced in the earlier part of his career by Art Nouveau was Omar Ramsden (1873–1939) who originally worked for a jeweller; but while attending evening classes he met Alwyn Carr, with whom he afterwards collaborated in the designing and making of gold and silver plate. Their masterpiece is a monstrance in silver gilt decorated with plaques of enamel, made in 1908 for Westminster Cathedral.

A year before Henry Wilson made the Brighton chalice, Meinrad Burch-Korrodi was born in Zurich. He studied for several years in London, Paris and New York, and in 1925 established his own workshop at Lucerne. A fellow student (though several years younger) at the Central School of Arts and Crafts, London, was Dunstan Pruden (b. 1906). These two outstanding goldsmiths are so different in their approach that it may be interesting to compare them. Burch is more original and inventive in his design, though not necessarily in his techniques. There is a panache about his work which has won him wide acclaim and many imitators. Dunstan Pruden has a more pious attitude towards the past, and has no use for innovation for its own sake. He believes that the perfecting of a good tradition has produced the greatest art, and that most new styles have evolved from new needs that have arisen or new materials and new techniques which have been developed. He has worked out his own methods, aiming always at being true to the character of the metal, and in this way has arrived at a style which is individual but within a traditional framework. Burch, carrying forward the Art Nouveau taste for enamel—some of his earlier chalices have lumpy knops not unlike Wilson's—has launched a fashion for altar vessels composed entirely, or almost entirely, of enamel. He has reduced his shapes to the utmost simplicity, relying on the brilliant colour and surface of the enamel to create an effect. He has gone rather too far in this direction, with the result that some of his vessels look rather like kitchen utensils or bathroom fittings; but he may have realized that his earlier style, with projecting bosses of semi-precious stones, might not be very practical or durable. He is more of a jeweller than Pruden, who on his side is more of a sculptor. Pruden does not like jewelled altar vessels, though he has sometimes used semi-precious stones, and he thinks that enamel should be used only as an enrichment. Both men work directly in the metal for their figurative work, so that in neither case does it look modelled; but Pruden's work looks hammered while Burch's often looks as though sheet metal has been bent, curled and cut with scissors like those ingenious paper dolls used in smart window dressing. Pruden's work is more massive and organic, Burch's is more elegant and wiry. Both have reaffirmed two facts which had almost been forgotten: that a chalice is a drinking-cup and that a ciborium is a bowl or dish for bread. Burch has recently been making chalices of the early *cantharus* type. with two handles. There is room for both styles in goldsmithing today, and the work of both men is in world-wide demand, being found in cathedrals, abbeys, universities, churches and seminaries in both hemispheres. Among Pruden's former pupils, Gerald Benney is generally regarded as the leading English designer of silver outside the scope of this book, but he has also received some important ecclesiastical commissions. Desmond Clen-Murphy is in no way inferior but has not yet achieved such wide recognition. Michael Murray has failed to make the best use of his talents by producing far too much work, some of it in base metals.

There are many creative goldsmiths at work today whom it is impossible to mention individually, but one may perhaps single out Hein Wimmer, Karl Schrage, Elizabeth Treskow, Roger Bonduel, Ilse von Drage, Toni Schneider Manzell and Fritz Schwerdt. Hein Wimmer has made a number of fine tabernacles in the casket form which is now favoured, and Karl Schrage seems to have found an answer to the problem of the thurible, a particularly difficult piece of church furnishing from the point of view of design. Monastic workshops have produced competent and often beautiful work, though there is sometimes a tendency to imitate current fashions instead of thinking out good basic workable shapes with appropriate ornaments. At Montserrat, for instance, the craftsmanship is better than some of the designs which are extravagant and impractical. One of the monks, when asked if a certain chalice was not difficult to lift (it had motifs like miniature railway buffers sprouting out of the knop) replied: "One can adapt oneself to it with practice." Enamel is used very lavishly at Montserrat, not only for vessels but also for such purposes as the decorative panel on the front of the high altar. Its current popularity is no doubt an expression of the need felt for some touch of warmth and richness to counteract the austerity of modern architecture; and as long as it is not abused by being thought of as material for an expensive and hardwearing picture, it has a legitimate place in liturgical art. Virgil Cantini is noted for his enamels in the U.S.A. The younger generation of goldsmiths often reflect the unrest of modern society in their work. Surfaces, instead of being smoothly burnished or gently hammered, are churned and furrowed into rugged textures, and are broken by scaly or irregularly chequered patterns.

Although the craft of the blacksmith is quite different from that of the worker in precious metals, this is the most appropriate place in which to consider the increasing use of wrought iron, not only for grilles, altar rails, candlesticks and light fittings, but also for crucifixes, statues and purely decorative work. Basil Spence designed a wrought iron screen in the form of a crown of thorns (executed by the Royal Engineers at Chatham) for the Gethsemane Chapel at Coventry Cathedral. As Mr John Russell has remarked, iron "had in itself a quality of raw nervous excitement" which seemed particularly in tune with the mood of the mid-twentieth century. Harry de Groot of Utrecht was a leader in this field, though his designs tended to be rather fantastic and fussy. Now every progressive church furnisher's show-room, once gleaming with brass, is black with wrought iron. Stainless steel is another material with immense possibilities apart from the appeal of its "contemporary" flavour. As long ago as the 1940's, Dunstan Pruden combined it with bronze to make a tabernacle for the church of St Pancras, Lewes, but it is unlikely to replace more traditional materials because it is relatively costly to work.

STAINED GLASS

Stained glass is perhaps the most generally admired and easily understood of all the liturgical arts. The force of its emotional impact and its unique property of translucent colour evoke a response even in people who are unfamiliar with its iconography and ignorant of its principles. During the period which we are considering, there was a tremendous demand for ecclesiastical glass especially in the English-speaking world, where so many medieval windows had been destroyed at home and where so many new churches were being built abroad.

The eighteenth century witnessed the nadir of this craft, and the year 1782 produced a landmark (or rather, as Mr Christopher Woodforde has described it, a low-water mark) in the form of the great west window of New College, Oxford, designed by Reynolds and painted in enamels by Thomas Jervais. It consists of a Nativity and a series of the Theological and Cardinal Virtues conceived in terms of easel painting, and having about as much relationship to the traditional craft of stained glass as a jigsaw puzzle has to a Byzantine mosaic. Although they were widely acclaimed, a few critical voices were raised, including those of Horace Walpole who referred to "Sir Joshua's washy Virtues" and Lord Torrington who called them "half-dressed languishing Harlots". These two connoisseurs were already admirers and collectors of medieval glass.

In the early nineteenth century, popular taste continued to favour reproductions of paintings. Raphael was held in the highest esteem, and in 1821 Joseph Backler painted a Resurrection in St Thomas's church, Dudley, Worcs., in which the figure of Christ was taken from Raphael's Transfiguration. The Victorian period at least had a more workmanlike approach to stained glass. The Gothic revival made people look with new eyes at medieval windows, and attempts were made to rediscover and adapt the methods of the Middle Ages. Charles Winston (1814–65) tried to improve the quality of stained glass by increasing its luminosity. His experiments were fostered by the firm of Whitefriars (which, in common with several other old-established companies, is still in operation), and samples of ancient glass were analysed. Similar aims were pursued by James Richard Clayton (1827–

1913), whose partner Alfred Bell (1832–95) founded a dynasty of which the fourth generation is active today. In spite of their researches, Clayton and Bell's glass (such as the windows in Bury St Edmunds and Truro cathedrals) was on the whole competent but dull. It was left to William Edward Chance, after years of trial and error, to produce the nearest approach to medieval glass. This was perfected in 1863 and was first used by Hardman and Co., another firm of church furnishers which is still flourishing. They had been pioneers in the Gothic revival, and many of Pugin's designs were carried out by them. Lloyd and Summerfield of Birmingham and Hartley's of Sunderland (later Hartley, Wood and Co.) soon began to produce "antique" types of glass, but although technical problems were solved, design continued to be governed by the principles of easel painting. The practice of reconstructing medieval methods without any understanding of the medieval spirit resulted in period pastiche with sentimental overtones, and the contribution which the leads should make to the design was not appreciated. At the Great Exhibition of 1851, prominent names (apart from that of Hardman) were those of O'Connor, Wailes, Hedgeland and Gibbs.

The Pre-Raphaelites, particularly the second wave consisting of Morris, Burne-Jones and Rossetti, tried to raise the standard of design. William Morris founded the firm of Morris and Co. in 1861. The other partners were Rossetti, Burne-Jones, Philip Webb, Madox Brown, Faulkner and Marshall. Their policy was to produce stained glass, textiles, wallpapers and furniture of good design and honest craftsmanship. Although Morris's medieval nostalgia was in its way as romantic and irrational as Pugin's, it differed in having for its ideal social reform instead of religious revival. Morris believed that the nineteenth century had lost touch with beauty because beauty could not exist where there was no pleasure in making. There was nothing for factory workers to enjoy in the mechanical labours of mass-production; and artists were discouraged because, instead of knowing themselves to be understood and appreciated by Everyman as in the Middle Ages, they now felt that their language was only intelligible to connoisseurs. The remedy, in Morris's view, lay partly in a return to individual craftsmanship and partly in encouraging artists to create their works for a general instead of a specialized public. Of course, the costs of production placed his wares beyond the means of the very people with whom he most wanted to make contact; but at least a breath of fresh air was introduced into the musty atmosphere of high Victorian aesthetics. To our eyes his compositions look just as crowded as any others of their period, although he paid lip-service to simplicity; but he had a remarkable talent for expressing the abundance of nature in terms of two-dimensional pattern. He often provided the backgrounds for figures by Burne-Jones who, after designing for a time for Whitefriars, ended by working exclusively for Morris. As they gained experience they learned to use the leads in their windows more expressively, and their most successful works in collaboration include those in Birmingham Cathedral, Christ Church, Oxford, and Easthampstead Church. Morris and Co. did not make their own glass, but were dependent on the best obtainable from manufacturers; and they saw nothing unsatisfactory in artists designing for a medium with which they were technically unfamiliar.

Contemporary with the Pre-Raphaelites but more conventional were Nathaniel Hubert Westlake (1833–1921) who was responsible for windows in Worcester cathedral and the churches of St John the Baptist, Brighton, the Sacred Heart, Hove, and St Philip Neri, Arundel: Charles Eames Kempe (1837–1907) whose many commissions included the choir of Bury St Edmund's Cathedral: and Henry Holiday (1839–1927) who was much in demand abroad, his masterpiece being the glass in the Rhinelander Memorial

Church of the Holy Trinity, New York. Much of the work of this period reflects Pre-Raphaelite mannerisms, and stained glass in general was still thought of in pictorial terms.

On the continent of Europe the situation was not dissimilar. In Germany, stained glass became an industry with results that made "Munich" a term of reproach. In France, Ingres and Delacroix designed windows for the Chapel Royal at Dreux, but few of the *peintres-verriers* who exhibited at the Paris Exhibition of 1855 made a lasting reputation. The only ones who are remembered today are Alfred Gerente (1821–68), originally a sculptor, who took over his dead brother Henri's atelier and exported work all over Europe: Adolphe Napoléon Didron (1806–67) and his nephew Edouard-Amedée Didron (1836–1902): and Antoine Lusson, who conducted a flourishing workshop at Le Mans between 1850 and 1872. A phenomenal case was that of the Abbé Deligny who, between 1860 and 1867, filled the windows of two churches in the department of Oise (Rémy and Jonquières) with naïve geometrical symbols which anticipate mid-twentieth-century work. Pauline Peugniez has called him *"Le Douanier Rousseau de la peinture sur verre"*. Large quantities of European glass were shipped across the Atlantic, for John La Farge was the only American artist to produce designs of comparable quality. His work was influenced by the Pre-Raphaelites, whom he sometimes excelled. It was not until the turn of the century that the craft of stained glass was practised seriously in the United States, and even then it followed existing patterns for several decades.

In the generations following the Pre-Raphaelites we find Christopher Whall (1850–1924) active in the Lady Chapel of Gloucester Cathedral and the south transept of Canterbury Cathedral. He was a good craftsman although he was chained to the pictorial tradition. His influence can still be traced in the work of living artists such as Joseph Nuttgens. Louis

Davis (1861–1941) might be called the last of the Pre-Raphael-ites, but he added an interesting personal contribution to his windows in Dublin Cathedral, Paisley Abbey and the English Church in Stockholm. The architect Sir John Ninian Comper (1864–1960), remembered more for his decoration of churches than for his actual buildings, designed stained glass as well as altars, statues, vestments, hangings, plate and every kind of church fitting. He was the most comprehensive medieval revivalist since Pugin, but his mood was less solemn and mysterious, and he did not scruple to mix Classic elements with Gothic. He stands in relation to Pugin rather as Rococo does to Baroque. His décor contrived to be at the same time opulent and exquisite, pretty and elegant. It was a kind of Edwardian dream of the Middle Ages, its pink and white and gold clearly visible in the daylight admitted by windows which contained a high proportion of clear glass. His tasteful pastiches created ecclesiastical fashions without making any real contribution to Christian art.

The transition into the twentieth century was not marked by any immediate change of style. Douglas Strachan (1875–1950) was prominent in Scotland where he provided windows for St Machar's Cathedral and King's College Chapel, Aberdeen. James Hogan (1883–1948) was much favoured in the United States. His windows may be seen in St Thomas's Church, New York, and the Church of the Heavenly Rest, New York; but Liverpool Cathedral offers an array of his glass which amounts to a retrospective exhibition, for it contains work which spans the greater part of his career. Martin Travers (1886–1948), as befitted a pupil of Comper, designed not only glass but all kinds of church fittings from altars and reredoses to crucifixes and candlesticks; but his inclination was towards Baroque and Rococo rather than Gothic. All his glass was made for Whitefriars, and the development of his style can be followed in

St Andrew's Church, Catford, London, where the windows date from 1921 to 1937. Other pupils of Comper, such as Geoffrey and Christopher Webb, were strongly influenced by their master. Areas of uncoloured glass were increasingly employed, especially by A. K. Nicholson, G. E. R. Smith and Reginald Bell.

It was from an unexpected quarter that a new wind began to blow. Sarah Purser (1849–1943) was an Irish portrait painter who presided over a monthly salon in her Dublin house. She was persuaded by Edward Martyn, who had been campaigning for the employment of artists instead of tradesmen in churches, to open a studio for the teaching of stained glass techniques. At first the instructors (Christopher Whall and his chief assistant A. E. Child) were English; but before the century was very far advanced, it became apparent that the new school had qualities which were lacking on the other side of the Irish Sea. Dublin artists, less affected by the "greenery-yallery" tradition and the languors of Burne-Jones, were turning out work which was richer in colour and more vigorous in line than that of their English counterparts. *An Túr Gloine* (The Tower of Glass) was a co-operative enterprise which provided craftsmen with studios and equipment, and it was one of the two main centres of production in Dublin. Michael Healey (b. 1873) worked there from 1903 until his death in 1941. He was a deeply religious man whose retiring disposition and slow but sure development caused him to be rather overshadowed by the more meteoric figure of Harry Clarke (1889–1931), whose studio was the other important focus of activity. Harry Clarke began his training in the firm founded by his father Joshua in 1886. This was not, incidentally, the oldest family business in Dublin, for the Earley Studios had been in existence since 1852, and craftsmen of the same name are still in operation. A turning point in the evolution of Harry Clarke's style was a visit to Chartres in 1914. He enjoyed an almost immediate success, and glass from his studios was not only in demand in his native country, but was sent all over the world. In the same way that Braque, though a less spectacular character, was just as much an innovator as Picasso, the modest Michael Healey was as much a pioneer in his way as Harry Clarke. Both men irradiated their colours by allowing light to shine through pinpoints eaten by acid, and it may have been Healey who originated the technique. Successive Bishops of Clonfert, with their see at Loughrea, County Galway, were among the first patrons of this Irish Renaissance. Michael Healey's work may be found there in the cathedral and in numerous other Irish churches and chapels including the Catholic Cathedral, Letterkenny, County Donegal; the Augustinian Church, Thomas Street, Dublin; and Clongowes College Chapel, County Kildare. Harry Clarke's comparatively early death did not end the flow of works from his studio, which was carried on by relatives and associates and is still in production. Some of his own ensembles can be seen in the Honan Hostel Chapel, Cork, and the Catholic churches of Carrickmacross, County Monaghan; Ballinrobe, County Mayo, and Timoleague, County Cork.

The most celebrated of all names in Irish stained glass is that of Evie Hone (1894–1955). Her working life in this medium was comparatively brief, for, as we have seen in the chapter on painting, she began her career as a painter and it was not until 1933 that she produced her first windows. In her earlier paintings she had been influenced by the Cubists, but her colour was deeper and richer. When she turned to glass it was from Rouault that she first sought inspiration. She worked with Michael Healey at the Tower of Glass and learned a great deal from him on the practical side, but she rejected the pinpointing technique. By the 1940's she had gained more assurance and her style became more personal. She aimed at a greater simplification than Clarke and Healey, attached more importance to the abstract patterns formed by the leads, and dispensed with ornamental borders and other irrelevant decoration. The result is less precious but more monumental, less hieratic but more directly expressive. Instead of sparkling like jewels, her colours transmit a lambent glow. She has been somewhat over praised by connoisseurs and critics, and rather unfairly criticized by some members of her own profession who regarded her as almost an amateur, because she had not been apprenticed to the craft in her youth. Her sense of scale has been questioned and it is, I think, true to say that she treated each window as an object in its own right, without due consideration for the architectural setting. Details, in themselves admirable, do not always build up to a satisfying unity in her larger compositions; but she must be credited with having spring-cleaned her craft of an accumulation of fustian while retaining all its sense of mystery. She has had a profound influence on younger artists such as Patrick Pollen (b. 1927), who was so impressed by her Eton window that he went to work with her in Dublin, and continues to produce glass in a similar tradition at his studio in *An Túr Gloine*. Besides the east window in Eton College Chapel, and another in St Michael's Church, Highgate, London, Evie Hone's major undertakings included ensembles in St Stanislaus College, Tullamore, County Offaly, and St Mary's Church, Kingscourt, County Cavan.

Evie Hone has not been the only member of her sex to achieve success as a stained glass artist. Wilhelmina Geddes (1888–1955) was more craftsmanlike in her approach, but the very personal technique which she used with such success was not one to be universally recommended. It was her practice to cover the whole surface of the glass with thin washes of paint so that her vigorous wiry line would not be vitiated by glare. She was an artist of great integrity. Like the Pre-Raphaelites she was very literal about such details as the age of Isaac when he was about to be sacrificed, a point which she verified by adding up the age references in the Book of Genesis; but this did not hamper the breadth and power of her conceptions, which did not follow the traditional patterns of Christian iconography. Her splendid Moses, unfortunately lost in an air-raid on Belfast, was no stock figure tricked out with long beard and tables of the law, but a real tribal leader. Much of her best work is in Church of Ireland and Presbyterian churches in Ireland, but there is a Crucifixion in St Luke's Church, Wallsend, a St Christopher in Laleham Church, near Staines, Middlesex, and a memorial window to King Albert of the Belgians presented to Ypres Cathedral in 1938 by the British Army and Air Force. Other well-known Irish names are those of Ethel Mary Rhind (d. 1952), who worked at *An Túr Gloine* from 1908: Beatrice Glenavy, who has made a number of windows in Ireland although she is primarily a painter: and Catherine O'Brien, who is the present owner of the Tower of Glass. In England, Moira Forsyth (b. 1905) has carried out commissions in many important buildings including Norwich and Guildford cathedrals and Eton College Chapel. She has evolved a style of painting in which a free cross hatching traps and filters the light without killing its brilliance.

Among the first signs of a revival on the Continent of Europe were Wyspianski's windows (1896) in the Franciscan church at Cracow, and those of Ferdinand Hodler (1853–1918) in Swiss churches. Hodler and other Swiss artists were influenced, about the turn of the century, by the English artist Holiday. Marcel Poncet's work at St Paul's in Geneva (1915) is also worthy of mention. Alexandre Cingria filled a number of Swiss churches including Notre-Dame, Geneva, and the parish church of Bulle, Fribourg, with his Baroque visions interpreted in glass. He did not try to force his spontaneous, dramatic style into the restricting mould of glass and lead, but somehow seemed to bend the intractable medium to his will. He often used flashed glass, sometimes with mirror glass "sandwiched" between the outer layers. He could scarcely have been more different from the classic Maurice Denis, who was the first important artist of the twentieth century to design glass in France.

It was not until after the First World War that Denis and Georges Desvallières started their school of sacred art, but Denis had designed windows for the church of Notre-Dame at Vésinet (Seine-et-Oise) as early as 1901. He had to wait until 1916 before he was given another ecclesiastical commission at St Paul's in Geneva, for although his style looks tame enough today, it was sufficiently unlike the fussy designs of the nineteenth century revivalists to cause disquiet in clerical circles. His air of primitive simplicity inspired by Giotto and Fra Angelico, his patches of flat local colour derived from the Pont Aven School, his habit of incorporating figures in modern dress in his religious compositions, his use of his wife and children as models for the Holy Family instead of idealized "devotional" types, all combined to make him *persona non grata* in the eyes of ecclesiastical patrons; and for some years his only outlet was in his own private oratory, where he decorated the apse with a window based on a theme from the hymn *Verbum Supernum*. However, when the church of Notre-Dame at Le Raincy was built in 1922–3, he was the only important French painter with experience in glass, and furthermore he had collaborated with the architect (Auguste Perret) in the decoration of the Champs Elysées Theatre ten years previously. He was therefore chosen to design the cage of stained glass which caused this revolutionary church to be described as "the Sainte-Chapelle of reinforced concrete". His associate Georges Desvallières also provided cartoons for glass (in the Ossuaire at Douaumont, 1927) which were executed by Jean Hébert Stevens; and among the first windows which could be called modern—although they no longer look very startling—one must include those in the church of Le Saint

Esprit, Avenue Dausmenil, Paris (built 1934), which were the result of a collaboration between Louis Barillet and Jacques le Chevallier. Barillet also collaborated with Théodore Hanssen, and his work may be seen in many cathedrals and churches, including Notre-Dame at Montligeon and the cathedral of Luxembourg.

At the International Paris Exhibition in 1937 there was a "Pavillon de Vitrail", and the Pontifical Pavilion housed an exhibition of glass destined for the nave windows of Notre-Dame de Paris. Twelve artists had been entrusted with this project under the direction of Jean Hébert Stevens. The members of the team were Fr Pierre Couturier O.P. (who had been one of the first group of students at Les Ateliers d'Art Sacré), Louis Barillet, Jacques le Chevallier, J. J. Gruber, J. K. Ray, P. Louzier, J. Rinuy, Valentine Reyre, F. Gaudier, Max Ingrand, Louis Mazetier and Pauline Peugniez. Some of these names have become famous while others are almost forgotten, and some of the windows which they produced were good while others were indifferent; but the Inspectorate of Historic Monuments has continued to pursue a policy of replacing poor nineteenth-century glass in historic buildings with windows by modern artists. Sometimes the results are harmonious and successful; but occasionally they are disastrous, as in the basilica of Saint-Michel at Bordeaux which contains some poor glass by Gaudin and some execrable glass by Couturat. The ancient church of Saint-Pierre at Montmartre has not fared much better at the hands of Max Ingrand, who seems to be a favourite of the Beaux Arts, for in the last twenty-five years his studios have covered acres of window-space with meretricious productions which cannot possibly retain any validity beyond the present period.

In the Pavillon du Vitrail at the 1937 Paris Exhibition, one of the items on show was a St Christopher window exhibited by A. Labouret. It was an example of a technique which he and Pierre Chaudière (who had been working with him for over thirty years on the restoration of glass in historic monuments) had developed in the early 1930's. Labouret had been searching for a method which would combine the strength and durability of modern materials with the splendour and colour found in ancient glass; and from their experiments had emerged the technique known as *dalles de verre*, in which slabs of glass which may be as much as $2\frac{1}{2}$ inches in thickness are set in a framework of cement reinforced with an armature of wire or steel bars. Of course, this is not really a new idea, but a reversion to primitive practice. The earliest windows consisted of small pieces of glass set in clay, mortar, wood, alabaster or marble. They were used in Byzantine churches as early as the sixth century, and in Muslim mosques from the seventh century onward. The *dalles de verre* technique has advantages and disadvantages. It is cheaper to produce than most respectable leaded glass, it is effective for abstract designs, and it is useful in built-up areas where the light is poor, because the facets (obtained by chipping the thick glass) act as reflectors. Rich glowing colours can be achieved because of the depth of the glass, but the appearance on the outside is rather blind and dead. It is a medium only suited to simple, broad, vigorous design, and it does not lend itself to lettering or the sort of detail that was attempted in Labouret's 1937 exhibit.

Two years before this International Exhibition, the periodical *L'Art Sacré*, which was destined to exert considerable influence, was founded by Joseph Pichard. From 1937 until 1954 it was directed by Fr Couturier and Fr Régamey, both Dominicans. During the war, Couturier was in the United States where he drew inspiration from the great American collections, and was in touch with Maritain, Focillon, Lèger and Chagall. On his return to France, he found a renewed activity stirring in the arts. New glass workshops had opened after the war, including those of Max Ingrand in Paris and

J. Simon at Rheims. Louis Barillet had left his atelier to his son Jean, and Jean Hébert Stevens had handed on the family tradition to his daughter Adeline and her husband Paul Bony, who were joined by Jacques Bony and Maurice Rocher. In 1946, Fr Couturier was appointed a sort of *maître d'œuvres* to direct operations at the Church of Notre-Dame de Toutes Grâces which was being built at Assy (Haute Savoie). This church had been begun on the initiative of Canon Devamey as long ago as 1937, but had been interrupted by the war. Marguerite Huré had completed the crypt windows in 1938, and when work was recommenced Fr Couturier was able to call upon the services of Rouault, Bazaine, Bercot, Brianchon, Paul Bony and Adeline Hébert-Stevens for the design and execution of stained glass, besides being responsible for some of the work himself. Although the actual building at Assy (designed by Novarina who was addicted to "picturesque" Savoyard styles) is not particularly praiseworthy either as architecture or as a setting for the liturgy, the whole project was a magnificent gesture. Notre-Dame de Toutes Grâces was the first post-war French church to which major artists made such an important contribution. It may have lacked unity but it was a source of pride, encouragement and inspiration to the whole Church.

One of the distinguished artists who helped to decorate Notre-Dame de Toutes Grâces was Matisse; and in 1947 he embarked upon the project which he himself regarded as the culmination of his whole life's work and "in spite of all its imperfections" his masterpiece. The story of how he undertook to design a chapel for the Dominican sisters at Vence has already entered the category of legend. What is particularly relevant here is the fact that the whole idea originated in a little water colour design painted by Sœur Jacques, a member of the community who had once nursed Matisse and subsequently visited him. When he was shown this sketch, Matisse was attracted by its freshness and simplicity, and offered to have it executed in stained glass for the new chapel which the sisters had in mind. At this stage neither he nor anyone else envisaged that in the end he would make himself responsible for the entire chapel from the building itself to the altar cloths and candlesticks, an undertaking which occupied him for four years. Although he was old and in failing health, he took infinite pains with every detail, ignoring the jeers of Picasso and other *incroyants*. He made three sets of full scale coloured cartoons for the windows before he was satisfied, aiming all the time at greater simplification; and his ultimate success is due partly to the fact that he did not prepare elaborate designs on a drawing-board but cut out the shapes in coloured paper. This gave them a directness and simplicity which made them readily adaptable to be cut out in a similar way in coloured glass. The disadvantages which result when an artist's ideal conception is translated into a craftsman's practical realization are therefore less glaring than they might be; and Paul Bony (who also carried out Rouault's designs at Assy) deserves praise for his sympathetic execution.

Matisse was primarily a great decorative artist, and the windows, like everything else at Vence, are decorative rather than profound; yet the whole chapel, slight though it is, deserves at least some of the extravagant praise that has been lavished on it. It achieves significance by virtue of its unique homogeneity, and in this respect it may be contrasted favourably with buildings like Coventry Cathedral, which are collections of unrelated works of art. (It is only fair to state that this effect was not an accident at Coventry, but the architect's intention. Basil Spence's plan was for a cathedral "like a plain jewel casket with many jewels inside".) The colour scheme of the Vence glass, which is restricted to ultramarine, gold and blue-green, allows a play of light on the white walls which is both calm and joyful; and the pattern of gold chestnut flowers expanding in the window behind the altar (although perhaps rather distracting) has an upward movement which suggests prayer and sacrifice.

Among artists of the first rank who have designed stained glass in the present century, the most successful in my opinion was Léger. For Novarina's Church of the Sacred Heart at Audincourt (Doubs), built in 1954, he provided a magnificent clerestory in the form of a continuous frieze of seventeen windows round the U-shaped sanctuary and nave. Brilliantly executed in slab glass and concrete by Jean Barillet, they are surely the finest expressions of this technique to date. Léger's bold, vigorous, simple style, with its heavy outlines and pure bright colours, proved readily adaptable to *dalles de verre*. To describe stained glass in terms of precious stones has become a cliché, but the windows at Audincourt really are sapphire and emerald and topaz, ruby and lapiz and gold. Their theme is the instruments of the passion, and in the same church Jean Bazaine has designed impressive walls of abstract glass (also executed by Barillet) for the baptistery. Another example of Léger's glass (representing the marriage feast at Cana) may be seen in the Swiss church of Courfaivre (1954).

Braque's style is perhaps too subtle to be translated into stained glass and his windows in the church of Varengeville (Seine Maritime) and the nearby chapel of Saint-Dominique are not in the same class as Léger's, although they were skilfully executed by Paul Bony. The glass designed by Chagall for Metz Cathedral and the new synagogue in Jerusalem is so seductive in colouring that one is almost bemused into overlooking its weaknesses. His characteristic style of suspending objects in space without attempting to resolve their spatial relationships is utterly unsuited to the medium, and the *folklorique* quality of his images, valid enough for some forms of religious art such as processional statues or domestic icons, is not sufficiently serious for anything so permanent as stained glass. Manessier has designed some good abstract glass, including windows in the old church of Les Brezeux (Doubs), installed in 1952: St Peter's at Arles-Trinquetaille (Bouches-du-Rhône), built in 1954: and Sainte-Thérèse, Hem (Nord), built in 1958. Le Corbusier disliked both the leaded and *dalles de verre* types of stained glass. For the windows at Notre-Dame-du-Haut, Ronchamp (Vosges), built in 1955, he used simple brush drawings fired on transparent glass, which he likes to call *vitrages* rather than *vitraux*.

In 1956 an exhibition called "Églises de France Reconstruites" was held in the Musée d'Art Moderne, Paris, and it was possible to see side by side work by Jacques le Chevallier, Jean Barillet, Maurice Rocher, Max Ingrand, Pierre Chevalley, François Chapuis, Gérard Lardeur and Claude Blanchet. One of the most prolific ateliers in recent times has been that of Gabriel Loire, who has worked for more than thirty-five years almost in the shadow of Chartres Cathedral. His windows in slab glass and concrete have travelled to places as far apart as the South German town of Mannheim and Galveston, Texas (partly, one suspects, for economic reasons, for his fees are highly competitive) but he is inclined to push his virtuosity too far. There is, I suppose, no reason why stained glass should not be used for structural purposes as well as for windows—after all, the walls of some Gothic churches were almost entirely composed of glass; but the cupola made up of small panels of coloured glass in the Carmelite chapel at Avranches (Manche) and the elliptical apse representing Christ in Majesty in the chapel of the Oblates of Mary at Portmain (Mayenne) seem to me to be in doubtful taste. In the church of Our Lady of Consolation, Hyères (Var) built in 1955, sculpture by Lambert Rücki is set into the outside of windows by Gabriel Loire. Léon Zack's thin colours and cobwebby leads at Notre-Dame des Pauvres, Issy (Seine) prevent very little light from entering the church, which was built in 1952. Although lacking in the richness that is traditionally associated with stained glass,

Zack's work—which may also be seen in the churches of Saint-Bernard, Reyersviller (Moselle), and the Sacred Heart, Mulhouse (Haut-Rhin)—is a relief from the turbid compositions of Max Ingrand. It is an unfortunate fact that at the present time French churches are being flooded with abstract glass which has no more merit than the pictorial glass of the nineteenth century; but because it looks "modern" and inoffensive, it is accepted with uncritical enthusiasm. A parish priest to whom I voiced this complaint declared that it is difficult to adopt a positive attitude with most stained glass practitioners, who automatically assume that all clerical patrons are ignorant and old-fashioned. In cases where funds will not allow a reputable artist to be commissioned, it would surely be better to make do with plain glass than to encourage a new kind of *bondieuserie* for the twenty-first century to sneer at and demolish.

Recent developments outside France include the researches of the Belgian artist Michel Martens, who has produced both abstract and representational work of high quality. His "Canticle of the Sun" in the Poor Clares' Convent at Ostend, and his "Heavenly Jerusalem" in Notre Dame College, Antwerp, bear comparison with any leaded glass of their period. Since 1962 Martens has been engaged in technical experiments resulting in compositions which he calls *Tableaux de verre*. In these he combines the transparency of leaded glass with the depth of slab glass by means of a system of laminated inlays, in which each layer preserves its identity while at the same time contributing to the general effect, rather like the parts in polyphony. In Switzerland, Hans Stocker is outstanding, though one might object to the glare produced by his huge window behind the altar of Our Lady of Solothurn near Berne (1951–2).

It was perhaps Elisabeth Coester's work in Otto Bartnung's steel and glass church in Cologne (1928) that set a fashion for entire walls of glass in German churches. Among the most striking of these are Dominikus Böhm's side wall of grey-green glass with its pattern of plant forms executed by Heinz Bienfeld in Maria Königin, Cologne-Marienburg (1954): and Georg Meistermann's great spiral composition for the façade of Holy Cross Church, Bottrop, Westphalia (1957). Much of the slab glass and concrete used in Germany (where it is called *Betonglas*) is imported from Gabriel Loire's workshops, but some of it is of German design, such as Boris Kleint's fine wall in St Mauritius, Saarbrücken.

Emile Mâle said that "Le vitrail est l'art des pays sans soleil." We might therefore expect to find Scandinavia rich in stained glass; but in fact many northern churches seem rather fortress-like with comparatively few windows (because for several months of the year artificial light is nearly always necessary) while in others such as the Technical University Chapel, Otaniemi, Helsinki, where forest trees provide a background for the altar, we find an imaginative use of clear glass. *Dalles de verre* were developed in Sweden by Ralph Bergholtz who, with his colleague Jan Brazda, worked out a "ceramic" treatment of glass. The purpose of this was to eliminate transparency without sacrificing translucency. The windows made by Bergholtz for the Kärleken Church, Halmstad, have a surface of small irregular lenses which diffuse light and add radiance. The glass font in this church was made by the same artist. The upper part forms the receptacle for baptismal water while the lower part is filled with water which reflects the windows. Bergholtz's glass may also be seen in the Hägersten Church, Stockholm. Bo Beskow's work (notably in the cathedral of Skara) has a rather folksy quality. He has tried to recapture the qualities of primitive glass, but admits that the processes to which he has subjected his material in an attempt to give it more life have robbed it to some extent of its colour and brilliance. Another Swedish artist of international reputation is Einar Forseth. His work in the Nicolaikyrkan in Halmstad (1954–5) combines a fairly traditional design with a somewhat arbitrary use of colour. His painting in the 1950's contains echoes of Picasso's *Demoiselles d'Avignon* period, and this influence is still strong in the windows (representing the bringing of the Gospel to Sweden by English missionaries) which he made as a personal gift to Coventry Cathedral in 1961–2.

Erwin Bossanyi, although born in Hungary in 1891, is a naturalized British citizen. He is probably best known for his panel of "The Angel blesses the women washing clothes" in the Tate Gallery (1937–42), but he also made the Unity and Peace window in the south transept of Canterbury Cathedral. The first windows of slab glass and concrete installed in England were made in France for Christ Church, Coventry, in 1956. They were the work of Pierre Fourmaintraux (b. 1897) who later joined the firm of Whitefriars. His work is a feature of many British churches (such as St Aidan's, East Acton) and has been widely exported. Dom Charles Norris (born 1909) of Buckfast Abbey has also developed this technique. Among younger English artists, Patrick Reyntiens (b. 1925) has won considerable acclaim as a result of his collaboration with John Piper. This has been one of the most successful examples of a relationship which by its nature is beset with pitfalls. Like Jean Barillet who carried out Léger's designs at Audincourt, the craftsman in this case is an artist in his own right and has both designed and executed glass in a number of churches and chapels, including the parish church of St Leonards-on-Sea, the Lady Chapel of Holy Cross, Hucknall, Notts, and St Anne's, Leyland, Lancs; but these commissions have not attracted so much publicity as work carried out to the designs of John Piper, which includes the resplendent galaxy of 198 lights in the baptistery at Coventry Cathedral, the "Attributes of Christ" in Oundle College Chapel, the "Instruments of the Passion" in St Andrew's Church, Plymouth, and windows in Eton College Chapel and Llandaff Cathedral. Whether this work is purely abstract or a form of representation marked by powerful flowing rhythms, design and execution seem to have been fused into an indivisible compound. Piper and Reyntiens are at present engaged on panels in *dalles de verre* for the lantern of the Catholic cathedral at Liverpool.

It was Coventry Cathedral that made the reputations of Geoffrey Clarke (b. 1924) and Keith New (b. 1926) who were commissioned to share the design and execution of the nave windows with Laurence Lee while they were still his students (though they were qualified and the holders of scholarships) at the Royal College of Art. These windows contain recognizable symbols relating to man's progress from birth to eternal life, while Margaret Trahearne's glass in the nearby Chapel of Unity is purely abstract. Varied though it is, all the glass at Coventry is in the English romantic tradition; that of Philip Brown (b. 1925) reflects the influences of his Paris training (particularly Le Chevallier and Rocher) and is more in the mainstream of the Christian iconographic tradition. His major works are the Seven Sacraments in the church of St Ambrose, Speke, near Liverpool: the west window in the chapel of St Patrick's Open Air School, Hayling Island, Hants: and, in collaboration with his wife Gounil, a window in St John's Cathedral, Umtata, South Africa.

Although the engraving of glass is quite a different craft, it will be convenient to consider it at this point. It has become increasingly popular since John Hutton made his great transparent screen, aquiver with wingy mysteries, for Coventry Cathedral. Engraved glass had already been employed effectively for secular purposes by such craftsmen as Tapio Wirkkala in Finland, but it has now been realized that it is a decorative way of separating narthex from nave. Some examples seen, such as the work of Sister Erentraut O.S.B. in the chapel of the University Clinic, Münster, are indifferent, and Arthur Fleischmann (an insipid artist in any medium) has given us a horrible variant in perspex at St Aidan's Church, East Acton, London.

One should, perhaps, also mention the technique of gemmail, conceived in France about thirty years ago by Jean Crotti and developed with the aid of a young doctor, Roger Malherbe. It consists of thousands of particles of glass of every colour and shape—cubes, rods, splinters and flakes—suspended at all angles in a transparent medium and fired repeatedly over a period of months. Artists of the stature of Braque, Rouault and Picasso have praised it in lyrical terms, and have not only allowed their work to be reproduced but have added their signatures. The medium is capable of extremes of beauty and vulgarity. Looking at a gemmail can be like walking into the heart of a fire, a diamond, a sub-aqueous grotto; or it can be like being lost in a wilderness of boiled sweets. Some windows in this technique were made for a church in Brooklyn, New York, as early as 1947, but the process had not been perfected and they did not prove weather-resistant. On the whole, there is something about the technique which reminds one of the childhood wonders of pantomime scenery, and this makes it more suitable for civic, industrial or domestic decoration than for use in churches. A museum of gemmail and a school for gem-mistes (the name by which its practitioners are known) have been established at Tours, and an international prize was instituted in 1957 to encourage young artists to design in this medium.

Rather in the same class as gemmail (because of its "magical" associations) is a new art form which has not yet been employed in churches, but which may have future possibilities. I refer to luminous moving pictures resulting from optical and kinetic combinations projected on a chosen surface. This medium involves colour, light, form and motion, and it is possible to control the tempo so that a given sequence unfolds as slowly as a flower, plays gently like a fountain or explodes in a shower of stars like a firework. A process demonstrated by John Healey in London in 1964 produced effects of great beauty which could be projected to any size from that of a postcard to that of an entire wall. The inventor believed that his images might prove acceptable aids to prayer and meditation.

TEXTILES

The origin and significance of the liturgical vestments are too well known to need reiteration here, but a few words about the history of the more important garments may help us to place recent developments in their true perspective.

The cope has retained its semicircular form since it first came into use in the eleventh century but, when the hood ceased to be worn during outdoor ceremonies or in cold draughty choirs, it tended to become a flat semicircular or triangular ornament. The alb, dalmatic and tunicle have varied little in shape though their decoration has, like that of all the other vestments, reflected changes in style. Medieval albs, for instance, often had oblong patches of embroidery (apparels) on the hem at front, back and sleeves, and these were highly prized at the period of the Gothic revival. In modern times the Church of England has on the whole been more enthusiastic about them than the Catholic Church which was inclined to show a preference for lace. The Anglican Warham Guild Handbook of 1932 sternly remarked that lace destroyed dignity and grace "and further there is no English authority for it"; but apparels were "an immense improvement". It is the chasuble which has undergone the most drastic modifications. Derived from the paenula, a conical cloak with a hole for the head, it was originally an everyday garment and for more than a thousand years no cleric complained that it was inconvenient to wear. It was drawn up or folded on each side to leave the arms free. It changed very little throughout the Middle Ages except that it received increasingly elaborate decoration from the ninth century onwards. The assumption that a voluminous garment became an encumbrance when the elevation of the Host was introduced into the Mass is not supported by an Andrea Pisano relief of the Eucharist on the campanile at Florence (perhaps designed by Giotto 1334–7) in which a priest is raising his arms freely in an antique type of chasuble.

Although the shape was sometimes elliptical, and the front and back were not always the same length, the chasuble did not undergo any serious mutilation until Renaissance times. When velvet and silk brocades were introduced and increasingly heavy embroidery became popular, it was gradually cut away at the sides until only enough was left to cover the front and back of the body; but this type of vestment, almost like a scapular, was not generally adopted until the sixteenth and seventeenth centuries. A good example, painted in meticulous detail, can be seen in Grünewald's *SS. Maurice and Erasmus* (*c.* 1584–5, Munich Pinakothek). The mutilated chasuble was never really authorized by the Church, and from time to time voices were raised in protest, including those of St Charles Borromeo in the sixteenth century and Cardinal Bona and Bishop du Saussay of Toul in the seventeenth century. Even in the eighteenth century the classical form was not abandoned entirely. In the diocese of Rouen it flourished until the French Revolution, and it was still used in Cistercian houses and in the cathedral of Angers.

At the beginning of the period which we are considering, the "cutaway" type of chasuble was the one in general use, differing only in minor details from one country to another. It fitted well enough with a Renaissance or Baroque background and certainly lent itself to much impressive decoration; but it was an ornament rather than a garment, and it made nonsense of certain traditional gestures (such as the lifting up of the side by the deacon and subdeacon at the incensing of the altar, and the raising of the hem by the server at the Consecration).

During the Gothic revival a travesty of the medieval vestment was invented which is still popular in some quarters under the misnomer of "Gothic". It was much skimpier than the classical garment for, instead of being tent-shaped, it had seams on the shoulders and was pointed at the back and front to give the impression of having been gathered up at the sides, whereas in fact it was still cut away to a considerable extent and the folds fell vertically instead of horizontally. It could not, of course, be as stiff as the so-called "fiddleback" or Roman chasuble, and was more comfortable to wear than the classical type as there was less weight on the arms. It also required less material.

Now there is nothing in the ecclesiastical law against having a chasuble so stiff that it looks as though it were cut out of metal, making the wearer look, as Viollet-le-Duc pointed out, like an enormous beetle; neither is there any commandment that forbids vertical folds. The only requirements that are essential and unchanging are that sacred vestments should be dignified and precious—not necessarily in the sense of being made of cloth of gold or encrusted with jewels, but in the sense of being the best that we can provide, of fine material and careful workmanship—and suitable for their liturgical function. It is a fact, however, that draped or enveloping garments falling in horizontal folds have always been regarded as more formal and noble than garments falling vertically from the shoulders. There are two reasons for this. In the first place, a draped garment demands a certain amount of poise and skill on the part of the wearer. In the second, a garment with vertical folds tends to cling to the body and emphasize its contours, thereby creating a sensual appeal; but a draped garment with horizontal folds tends to obscure the physical characteristics of the wearer and to focus attention on his office. There can be little doubt, therefore, that the classical type of garment looks more dignified and worthy of its function, and it may even contribute to the proper and reverent conduct of the liturgy by making the celebrant conscious of what he is wearing and why, and thus discouraging a hurried and scamped performance; but we should not insist on it on *archeological* grounds, for the Church is not an early Christian church or a Romanesque church or a Gothic church, but the mystical body of Christ living and renewing itself in every age.

As far as can be ascertained, the first chasuble to be worn in the Church of England was made by a Miss Marian Hughes for Mr Chamberlain, rector of St Thomas's, Oxford, in the 1840's. The red silk material came from two Oxford M.A. hoods sewn together, thereby reversing the post-Reformation practice of diverting sacred vestments to secular use.

The first Anglican church to use vestments in London was St Mary Magdalen, Munster Square, in 1864. In 1870 and again in 1877 the Privy Council ruled that the cope and surplice were the only legal vestments, but individual clergy continued to follow their own consciences, a situation which led to a great variety of practice. To end the confusion a subcommittee of bishops appointed by Convocation concluded in 1908 that the vestments prescribed by the First Prayer Book of Edward VI ("an alb plain with a vestment or cope") were permissible. Anglican clergy have usually preferred the Gothic revival type of chasuble, many of which were made by the Bethany Sisters of Lloyd Square, London, and the Society of St Margaret, East Grinstead, Sussex.

The form of chasuble now coming into more general use seems to be a development of the 1920's, probably as a result of the liturgical movement. French Dominicans and priests of the diocese of Moulins had worn chasubles described as "ample" during the lifetime of Dom Guéranger, but we do not know how close they were to the conical shape. In 1927 a convert clergyman named Roger Kynaston, who was also a painter, designed a set of vestments cut on classical lines for Blackfriars, Oxford. They were made from Assam silk handwoven by Valentine Kilbride of Ditchling Common, Sussex, who shortly after adopted a similar pattern when making vestments himself. Raymund James, who had previously been an advocate of the Gothic revival shape, also changed to this style. In the 1930's, Valentine Kilbride and Bernard Brocklehurst aimed at producing a material more suited to the shape of the classical chasuble than anything obtainable from the general textile trade. The result was woven from spun silk in relatively coarse thicknesses of thread, and it lent itself as readily as wool to folds and drapery which were at the same time soft and sculptural. This material, together with vestments made from it, is still being made at Ditchling, and the craft has spread to certain religious houses, notably Prinknash and Quarr. The conditions of handloom weaving are not conducive to large scale production, but the fact that materials of this kind are particularly suitable for ample vestments is gaining widespread recognition. Anyone who has woven and perhaps dyed the material is better able to assess the possibilities of its ultimate design. It may be objected that poor parishes cannot afford costly materials, but the difference in price between handwoven silk and mass-produced brocade is less than is commonly supposed. It is really a matter of priorities: many parishes could afford a few good essentials if they dispensed with a clutter of mediocre non-essentials.

One of the most celebrated centres of vestment making and design is the Sancta Klara Institute at Stans in Switzerland, supervised by Schwester Augustina Flüeler. This convent, founded in the seventeenth century, had made vestments before the French Revolution, but the tradition had been abandoned in the nineteenth century. A special crafts selection was organized in the girls' school in 1924, and the needlework class eventually became an atelier, no longer teaching but employing both religious and lay workers of expert standard. This workshop does not base its designs on any definite historical style, and it goes its own way little influenced by current trends. Its vestments are ample and dignified, and decoration is considered of secondary importance to cut and proportion, but some of them have the air of *haute couture* rather than of liturgical garments. Schwester Flüeler says that she only began handweaving because the Second World War made it difficult to obtain suitable materials. By experiment she discovered the effects of a combination of bright and matt threads, raised or coloured stripes and bands, which could not only rival the richness of Baroque brocades and damasks but could be woven in anticipation of the final cut of the vestment. She uses wool as well as silk in preference to artificial silk although this is not officially permitted, and one might question its wisdom from the point of view of durability; but it certainly looks virile and drapes handsomely. She has also sponsored the idea of white Mass vestments for Deacon and Subdeacon on all occasions, thereby obviating the expense of complete sets in all the liturgical colours. Other continental religious communities engaged in this craft with some success include the Benedictines of Vanves and the Dominicans of Cannes. Especially deserving of mention are the Benedictine monks of Montserrat in Spain, who have recently "rethought" their vestments, and are now weaving magnificently ample garments of great simplicity and dignity. Schwester Flüeler has also had a considerable influence in America. The close association of Belgium with the liturgical movement probably accounts for the fact that Belgian commercial church furnishers have been among the most active in sponsoring well cut vestments, although they were reluctant to forgo elaborate decoration.

Several celebrated artists have designed vestments, notably Matisse and Manessier. Those conceived by Matisse for the Rosary Chapel at Vence are, like Bernini's St Teresa, an example of religious art that walks on a tightrope. Both are only just saved by the genius of their creators, and by their unity with the setting. St Teresa is almost, but not quite, a vulgar exercise in overstatement: the Vence vestments are almost, but not quite, a set of theatrical costumes. They have been imitated with disastrous results. In too many churches vestments are appearing with bold abstract appliqué designs of a kind more suitable on the stage than in the sanctuary. Those of Josef and Franziska Mikl in Germany err in this direction, and those of Erna Schillig are notable for workmanship rather than design. Far more successful are those which depend for their effect on the cut, colour, texture and draping qualities of the materials used; yet here there is a possible danger, as in some of our new churches, of being afraid of any form of decoration and becoming too austere. It is suggested that, just as the splendour of kimonos shows to advantage in the bare rooms of Japanese houses, so magnificent vestments could be the jewels enriching some of our over-bleak interiors.

Before the advent of the Arts and Crafts Movement, the more important examples of ecclesiastical needlework were often designed by church architects, whose approach tended to be archeological. Riddels, dossals, altar frontals, testers, banners and kneelers were embroidered as well as vestments, and attempts were made to rival the intricacies of *opus anglicanum*; but the invention of aniline dyes led to such a wide range of colours being available that the temptation to use too many was irresistible. The Belgian firm of Grossé, founded in 1783, employed highly skilled embroiderers noted for their elaborate workmanship. Among their records is a description of a set of vestments of Gothic inspiration presented to the Bishop of Angers in 1884, which is in its way a *tour de force*. The mitre, with miniatures of the Bishop-saints of Angers designed by M. de Tracy of Ghent, took 465 days to embroider: 1,039 days were spent on the cope, and a single needlewoman was engaged on the stole for nearly four years. All the workers employed on the project stitched solidly for ten hours a day.

With the establishment of William Morris's factory at Merton, less imitative designs began to appear. Although most of Morris's products were tapestries or other woven textiles, some of his associates such as Philip Webb produced original designs for liturgical needlework. Morris always insisted on calling his tapestries "arras" because the name "tapestry" had become associated with manufactured materials. Burne-Jones often designed the figures while Philip Webb and Henry Dearle supplied the background and animals. Other artists who worked for Morris included Walter Crane and Byam Shaw. The "Adoration of the Magi" at Exeter College, Oxford, was one of the hangings made on the Merton looms.

The first American tapestry workshop was that of William Baumgarten, founded at Williamsbridge, New York, in 1893. Baumgarten brought over M. Foussadier, formerly master workman at the Royal Windsor tapestry works, and skilled craftsmen from France, mainly from Aubusson. Another important American workshop was that of the Herter looms, established in 1908. Albert Herter's ideas were rather like those of Morris, and he not only designed tapestries but actually wove them himself.

Throughout the nineteenth century and during the first third of the twentieth century, tapestry was almost certainly governed by the principles applicable to painting. It was forgotten that the purpose of tapestry is to furnish and adorn large flat areas, and that it should respect the wall by avoiding *trompe l'oeil* effects, distant perspectives and anything that creates a "hole" in the wall. More than anyone else, Jean Lurçat (b. 1892) has been responsible for restoring to tapestry the properties of a woven hanging rather than those of a substitute picture. Originally a painter, he became interested in murals in 1913 and in tapestry two years later; but he did not entirely abandon easel painting. From about 1938, influenced by the Apocalypse of Angers, he began to reinvigorate the craft with something of its medieval boldness by using coarser textures and a restricted scale of colours. The identity of the threads and the limitations which this placed on the composition were no longer smoothed over as in the woven productions of paintings which had for so long been admired. After the liberation of Paris in 1945, a group was formed called the "Association des Peintres-Cartonniers de Tapisserie". Among its earliest members, brought together by Denise Majorel and Lurçat himself, were Marc Saint-Saëns, Jean Picart le Doux, and Dom Robert. In 1947 Lurçat designed the Apocalypse tapestry for the church of Notre-Dame de Toutes Grâces at Assy.

Dom Robert (b. 1907) entered the Benedictine order in 1930. His first work "Summer" was woven in 1942, a year after Lurçat, while staying in the monastery of En Calcat (Tarn), had diverted his interest from the illumination of manuscripts to tapestry. Other works include a Visitation (1945), a Creation of Man (1946) and *Terribilis* (1946) which represents our Lady as the protectress of Dijon. His charming little animals and plants are in the true tradition of the *mille-fleurs* tapestries of the late fifteenth and early sixteenth centuries, but his fairytale madonnas and folksy patriarchs look rather frivolous for use as backcloths in the solemn play of the liturgy. A typical example may be seen in the Church of Notre-Dame de France, Leicester Square, London, where a figure that might well be Snow-White seems an unworthy personification of our Lady as pre-figured in the Book of Wisdom. Jean Olin's tapestries in St Martin, Holtswihr, St Joseph, Dijon, St Louis, Brest, and the seminary chapel at Walburg are more successful if only because they avoid this naïve prettiness.

When Léger designed his windows for the Church of the Sacred Heart, Audincourt (1955), he also provided a cartoon for the hanging in the sanctuary; and Rouault designed a tapestry, woven by Plasse Lacaisne, for the church of Sainte Thérèse, Hem (Nord), in 1958. Graham Sutherland's Christ in Majesty, which covers the east wall of Coventry Cathedral, was completed in 1962. It is the largest tapestry in the world. It lacks a true feeling for the character of the medium and the subject was not really sympathetic to a Romantic artist with Expressionist tendencies; but it is nevertheless a heroic conception which could not have been attempted by the archeologically minded and nostalgic designers of the nineteenth century. In scale alone, it can scarcely fail to dominate its setting.

Although there seems a considerable future for tapestry as a means of bringing warmth, colour and textural interest to walls which are so often bare, it may be objected that the space behind the altar is too distracting a position. Some hangings used in this way are not tapestries but needlework panels of one kind or another, such as Sybil D. Emerson's abstract hanging behind the altar in Pennsylvania State University Chapel, or Madame Nüte-Kammerer's large panel of Our Lady of Mercy in the apse of the University Clinic Chapel, Münster. Accomplished needlewomen capable of producing original designs are so numerous that one can only mention a few names at random. In England, there are Beryl Dean and Frances Parker. It is hard to choose between Anna-Lisa Odelquist and Marta Afzelius of Stockholm, the Sisters of Providence of Friedrichsburg, Münster, Sr Theodata of Uber Sarlgat and Sr M. Regina of Kloster

St Ursula, Augsburg. The English architect, George G. Pace, carries on the tradition of Comper, W. H. Randoll Blacking, F. C. Eden and many nineteenth-century architects when he designs frontals and kneelers for churches which he has planned.

MOSAIC

The nineteenth-century enthusiasm for medieval antiquities was responsible for a renewed interest in mosaic which, like stained glass and tapestry, continued throughout the greater part of our period to be valued only as an ingenious imitation of painting. The very characteristics which should give mosaic its special quality were eliminated. Instead of irregularly shaped tesserae set at varying angles to catch and reflect the light, we find neat little squares arranged with the precision of pieces in a child's box of bricks. Instead of broad, simple designs which would not strain the rigid nature of the materials, intricate details and carefully modulated tones were attempted. Sir Edward Poynter, for example, produced cartoons in exactly the same style as his paintings and had them reproduced flatly on the wall; and until comparatively recently, altar-pieces and mural decorations representing copies of favourite paintings such as the Sistine Madonna and Murillo's Immaculate Conception were common.

An exception was the work of Antoni Gaudí (1852–1926) in Barcelona. His mosaics, in their exploitation of fortuitous materials such as broken dolls, cups, bottles, tiles and plates, were heralds of Surrealism in the earliest years of the twentieth century. The pinnacles of the Sagrada Familia church are crowned by features in this medium.

Sanctuaries and vaults lined with mosaic became very popular after Westminster Cathedral had been decorated in this way by Robert Anning Bell, Christian Symons, Gilbert Pownall and others. Some commercial firms, such as Oppenheimer's of Dublin, specialized in this work. In 1921,

Gabriel Pippet devised an ambitious scheme in a Romano-Byzantine style for the Catholic Church at Droitwich, Worcs, and Maurice Josey with his assistant Frederick Oates worked on it for twelve years.

In France, this form of decoration was often chosen for important shrines, such as the basilica of Sacré Cœur and the Chapel of the Sisters of Charity in the Rue du Bac, Paris (where the incorrupt body of St Catherine Labouré is venerated), and the basilicas of Lourdes, Lisieux and Domrémy. The rich effect of gilt and colour, combined with the sentimental "devotional" treatment usually chosen, represented the early twentieth century's attempt to recapture for humble pilgrims the vision of Heaven evoked so much more splendidly by Baroque and Rococo interiors.

In the second and third decades of the century, Alexandre Cingria and Maurice Denis produced some designs for Swiss churches which were more in the tradition of Roman mosaics, and Gino Severini also brought a more original simplified approach to this medium (as in the church of St Peter Canisius, Fribourg).

In the 1950's, some of the foremost artists of the period designed mosaics for churches. These included Léger and Chagall at Assy, Lurçat at the Church of SS. Peter and Paul, Maubeuge (executed by Michel Schmidt), Bazaine at the Church of the Sacred Heart, Audincourt (executed by Gaudin) and Campigli in Italy. Barillet and other artists in stained glass sometimes practised this craft, and in fact some stained glass (such as the "lucent mosaic" made by the Cummings Studios in San Francisco, and the work of Richard Sussmüth in West Germany) could be classified as a form of mosaic. Einar Forseth's floor for the Chapel of Unity in Coventry Cathedral (1961–2) is more properly described as a design in inlaid marbles (executed by Cecil Whitehead). The Belgian artist Gilbert Swimberghe is half-way towards being a sculptor of reliefs. When he first began to work in mosaic in 1960 he used Venetian glass tesserae but, finding the medium uncongenial, he turned to stones, pebbles and cobbles. Italian mosaicists are masters of their craft but few of those engaged on ecclesiastical work (industrial design is another matter) have broken away from the imitative style of the nineteenth century. In Germany, Emile Sutor designed a curious mosaic statue for the Frauenfriedens-kirche, Frankfurt. It has a concrete kernel which August Wagner of Berlin covered with coloured glass cubes.

Interesting new developments are in progress in Central and South America, particularly in Mexico and Brazil where imaginative use is being made of volcanic rocks, seashells and other natural materials, sometimes on a vast scale. Many of these mosaics are on civic and industrial buildings (such as Diego Rivera's on the Olympic Stadium and Juan O'Gorman's on the University Library, Mexico City), but they are also being applied to ecclesiastical architecture. The work of José Chavez Morado and Enrique Valderrama deserves mention. In the United States Louisa Jenkins interprets religious subjects in this medium.

In England, Michael Leigh (b. 1906) does not approach mosaic with any pictorial misconceptions, although he is primarily a painter. His work has an authentic irregularity of surface, and he uses interesting and varied materials for his tesserae without attempting any inappropriate modula-tions of tone. Typical examples may be seen at the Carmelite Priory at Faversham, Kent. The most imposing ensemble of recent years, however, is the decoration of the Blessed Sacrament Chapel in Westminster Cathedral (1962) by Boris Anrep. Although it is a *tour de force*, especially for a man of such advanced age—he was born in 1883—one cannot regard it without a certain degree of disappointment. Anrep's earlier panel of Blessed Oliver Plunket, modest though it is in comparison, led one to expect that when offered such a rare and magnificent opportunity as the

Blessed Sacrament Chapel the artist would respond by producing a unique masterpiece. Boris Anrep is Russian by birth and Russian artists have, as we know, a much deeper respect for tradition than artists in Western Europe; but though he has drawn on the legacy of Byzantium, he has made the same sort of concession to naturalism that we find in the work of Russian artists who, from the time of Peter the Great onwards, tried to graft Western standards on to their own hallowed formulas. If the predominant impression of pink and gold reminds some spectators of the sugar-plum Edwardiana of Sir John Ninian Comper, it should be pointed out that there is classical precedent for this innocent colour scheme. The scale, too, is good, and the relation of parts to whole is well organized; but the vignette of St Peter's in the middle of the apse is of almost unbelievable vulgarity, and the setting of the tesserae throughout lacks life. Another of Anrep's religious works is the Vision of St John in the chapel of the Royal Military College, Sandhurst. He is really happier when designing pavements. He himself once told René McColl that he felt it was possible to reach a much greater degree of intimacy with the spectator from that angle: "to gaze downwards is an easy, natural gesture". Early in 1965 Justin Vulliamy, with the advice and co-operation of Boris Anrep, completed the mosaic decorations in the chapel of St Paul in Westminster Cathedral. As in The Blessed Sacrament Chapel, the formal elements are pleasant enough but the figures represent a compromise and there is a dreadful lion straight out of a Disney cartoon.

CERAMICS

Throughout the period under review, statuettes and plaques in porcelain and earthenware have been popular for domestic shrines. Some of the earlier examples have a period charm or the attractive naïveté of peasant art, while others are ambitious translations of "Old Masters" such as a jasper plaque of The Descent from the Cross (based on Rubens) made by Enoch Wood in 1779. Few of those produced in recent years have any artistic merit. Martin Travers (1886–1948) and other architects of his period liked to decorate their churches with copies of della Robbia plaques, which in their original form were terra cotta reliefs covered with tin enamel glazes.

Tiles have always been an important feature of architecture in countries subject to Moorish influence, and visitors to the Iberian peninsula will be familiar with the *azulejos* which, more often in Portugal than in Spain, represent religious subjects. They are also by extension prevalent in Brazil. A modern example is Cándido Portinari's huge decoration for the exterior of Niemeyer's Church of São Francisco at Pampulha. It was not until the nineteenth century that tiles were used extensively in the decoration of English churches. William Butterfield's addiction to them, both for walls and floors, is well illustrated in the church of All Saints, Margaret Street, London. The encaustic tiles made by Minton and Co. were much admired and there was a vogue for reproductions of Faenza and Palissy ware. Philip Webb (1831–1915) produced some of the more original designs for tiles.

Twentieth-century developments follow the pattern which we have already seen in the other sections of this chapter. Creative designs began to replace copies of classic works of art, and celebrated artists turned their attention to this medium. Outstanding examples are Léger's American War Memorial at Bastogne, Belgium (1950), and Matisse's black outline drawings fired on white faïence slabs at Vence (1951). Joan Miró has probably carried this art-form further than anyone else, but he has not produced any religious work.

It is impossible to enumerate all the competent ceramists at work in European churches, but one may mention Giulio Minoletti, Véronique Filozof, Florence Tournon-Branly and Françoise Bizette before devoting a little more space to Adam Kossowski (b. 1905) who is perhaps the most interesting of all. Of Polish birth and trained in Cracow, Warsaw and Rome, he has settled in England where typical examples of his work may be seen at St David's Cathedral, Cardiff, Downside Abbey, the Carmelite Priory, Aylesford, and the churches of St Ambrose, Speke, near Liverpool and St Aidan, East Acton, London. An indifferent draughtsman but a fine colourist, his Expressionist vision is best realized in ceramic panels of sculpturesque character. Teresa Fuller (b. 1900) on the other hand, is primarily a painter, and the altar-pieces and mural decorations on tiles to which she has lately devoted much of her time are logical developments of her charming earlier style of tempera painting with its Primitive Italianate atmosphere. Examples may be seen in Digby Stuart College, London, and the churches of St Lawrence, Edenbridge, Kent, St Aloysius, Oxford, and the Sacred Heart, Charlton Kings, Glos.

Ceramic materials are also widely used for more functional objects connected with the liturgy such as fonts and other receptacles for holy water. The sanctuary candlesticks at Coventry Cathedral (designed by Hans Coper) are made of pottery. Monastic workshops sometimes produce good work of this kind but in too many cases there is a tendency—understandable but regrettable—to cater for the tourist trade.

CONCLUSION

This book goes to press at a time when the pattern of worship is undergoing changes which are likely to be reflected in the Christian art of the future. Processes of this kind have always been at work in the Church, and with obvious exceptions such as Iconoclasm or the austere attitude of St Bernard, have usually added to the opportunities of the artist. For example, the rise of the cult of relics naturally led to a great demand for reliquaries and, in the late tenth century, produced a new architectural feature, the ambulatory or "clearway" allowing access to the absidal chapels in which relics were housed and venerated: and the medieval focusing of devotion on the physical presence of our Lord in the Eucharist led to the design of a new altar vessel, the monstrance.

At first sight it may appear that modern trends offer a negative outlook for artists. The preference for churches with an open plan, in which strong emphasis is placed on the high altar, discourages the provision of subsidiary chapels with their statues, altar-pieces, candlesticks and other fittings; Mass facing the people, and the ideal of consecrating hosts offered by the intending communicants, can hardly fail to contribute to the disappearance of the tabernacle from the altar of sacrifice (although of course some other safe place, such as an aumbry, must be provided for the reservation of the Blessed Sacrament); the movement away from the concept of the Eucharist as something to be kept and looked at rather than consumed may make the monstrance superfluous; the declared wish of certain bishops at the Second Vatican Council to exchange their gold and silver rings and pectoral crosses for ornaments of wood or base metal may modify this branch of the goldsmith's work; and the return to ample, flowing chasubles means that elaborate embroidery is no longer necessary or desirable.

All this does not mean that the architect will be the only artist still needed by the Church. We may, however, expect to see painting and sculpture become more integrated with structure as they were in Romanesque and early Gothic times; and a decline in the popularity of portable ornaments such as free-standing statues and framed pictures may be compensated by an increasing use of more organic forms of decoration such as mosaics and ceramic tiles and panels: and we may hope to see more discrimination in the choosing of altar vessels which are likely to be exposed to view during most of the Mass, instead of being hidden away in a taber-nacle.

We should remember that in the first flush of our enthu-siasm for liturgical reform we are liable to be over zealous, and the more dogmatic of our prescriptions may look just as exaggerated in a hundred years' time as those of the Ecclesiologists appear to us today. The emphasis on corporate worship should not blind us to the fact that private devotion fulfils an equally basic need in mankind and has a tradition just as venerable. We may dismiss all the hermits and solitaries in the Calendar as phenomena valid for their own times rather than ours, but we cannot overlook the fact that our Lord himself did not only participate in the worship of the temple and synagogue but also on many occasions "went apart to pray", "went up into a mountainside to pray", and "passed the whole night offering prayer to God". It is in work designed for private use that the artist enjoys the greatest freedom, for it is not covered by the Church's understandable restrictions on experimental (and perhaps ephemeral) forms of art in places of public worship. A number of artists whose work at one time found only private patrons are now not only accepted but in great demand for official commissions.

This leads us to the question of mass production, for many people who wish to have domestic shrines cannot (or think they cannot) afford original works of art. Their needs ought to be fulfilled and we must consider the best ways of doing this. In the first place, original work is not always as costly as the general public imagines, and it is always worth while to make inquiries. In the second place, articles produced to satisfy a popular demand need not be objectionable if they follow a good tradition. In the past they have often been very fine: one can point to such examples as the processional images of Catalonia and the Basque country, Mosan metalwork, Limoges enamels, Nottingham alabasters, peasant Baroque woodcarvings and the sort of icon sold at fairs in Central and Eastern Europe. Some materials should, I think, be excluded as unworthy, either because of their intrinsically unpleasant appearance or because they are so fragile that they soon become shabby: these include plastics and plaster of Paris. I do not think that any work of art can be *mass*-produced, however good the original design may be, because on such a scale the production passes out of control of the artist; furthermore, if artists are employed to make designs without knowing the problems involved in production, their ideas often look very promising on the drawing-board but literally do not work in practice, so that they have to be adapted by technicians. There are some media, however, in which it is possible to reproduce works of art in quantities, but the scale must be limited by the artist's capacity to keep the end product under his control. The most obvious examples are prints of various kinds (woodcuts, engravings, lithographs), cast metalwork and ceramics. Even after being repeated hundreds, and in some cases thousands of times, all of these remain in some sense original works of art because no two are exactly alike. The material used, the skill of the craftsmen concerned and the degree of finish all produce subtle variations.

There seems to be no way of breaking the vicious circle which operates in the supply of "objects of piety", an industry in which the standard of design at some levels seems lower than in almost any other. While rubbish is sold there will always be a market for it, and while there is a demand manufacturers (being human) will continue to supply it. It is true that in the shadow of Saint-Sulpice a new *bondieuserie* has risen up beside the old, but ugliness and distortion for their own sake are no better than candy colours and sentimental naturalism. An encouraging development of our time is the increasing tendency of architects to entrust work in their churches to the best artists they know instead of designing all the fittings themselves and leaving the execution to tradesmen, which was a common practice in the Victorian and Edwardian periods. One can only hope that if people are given more opportunities to become familiar with good work in new churches, exhibitions, books, periodicals and illustrated talks, they will begin to want it for themselves; for, in the words of Maritain, "the perception of the beautiful is related to knowledge".

Sources of the illustrations

1. By courtesy of Brighton Art Gallery. 2. Folkwang Museum, Essen. 3. Photograph by Peter Parkinson, by permission of the Borough Librarian, Bethnal Green. 4 & 10. By permission of the Director of the Tate Gallery, London. 5. Photograph by Deane and Miller. 8. Photograph A. C. Cooper Ltd, by courtesy of the Arts Council. 9. Teresa Fuller, Digby Stuart College, London. 11. David Jones, collection of the artist. 12. Private collection, by permission of the Executors, London. 13. By permission of the Bursar, Leeds University. 14. Cement and Concrete Association. 15. Henry Moore. 16. Arthur Pollen, collection of the artist, photograph by Francis Pollen. 17. Photograph by Raymond Wilson. 18. The author. 19. Photograph by Leonard von Matt in *Gold und Silberarbeiten aus der werkstatt Meinrad Burch-Korrodi*. 20. By kind permission of the Arts Council and the Very Rev. Superior, Jesuit Retreat House, Tullamore, Eire. 21, 22, 23 & 24. Details of photographs by G. E. Kidder Smith in *The New Churches of Europe* (Architectural Press, London). 25. John Piper. 27. Abbey of Montserrat, Spain. 28. Photograph by Lee Harley in 'Design Quarterly', Walker Art Centre, Minn. 29. Photograph by Eric Sutherland in 'Design Quarterly', Walker Art Centre, Minn. 30. Photograph A. C. Cooper Ltd. 31. Collection Rupert Nassauer, London, by permission of Mr Nassauer. 32. By permission of the Pallas Gallery, Albemarle Street, London, collection Lady Honor Svejdar, Dublin. 33. From a photograph by Luc Fournol and Daniel Frasnay, by courtesy of Galerie David et Garnier, Paris. 34. From a photograph in the review 'Werk', Winterthour. 35. Photograph J. S. Markiewicz. 36. From a photograph by G. E. Kidder Smith in *The New Churches of Europe* (Architectural Press, London). 37 & 38. Photographs by J. Sapanel, Marly-le-Roi, S & O, France. 39. Archives Photographiques, Paris.

SELECT BIBLIOGRAPHY

In this series: LESAGE, Robert: *Vestments and Church Furniture;* SYNDICUS, Eduard, S. J.: *Early Christian Art.*

ANSON, Peter: *Fashions in Church Furnishing*, London, Faith Press, and New York, Macmillan, 1960.

ARMITAGE, E. Liddell: *Stained Glass*, Newton Centre, Mass., Branford, and London, Allen, 1959.

BETJEMAN, John: *American's Guide to English Parish Churches*, New York, Obolensky, 1959 (English edn, *Collins' Guide to English Parish Churches*, London, Collins, 1958).

BOUYER, L.: *Liturgical Piety* (English edn, *Life and Liturgy*), Notre Dame, Ind., Univ. of Notre Dame Press, 1955, and London, Sheed and Ward, 1956.

BRODERICK, Robert C.: *Historic Churches of the United States*, New York, Funk and Wagnalls, 1958.

CETTO, Max: *Modern Architecture in Mexico*, New York, Praeger, 1961.

CLARK, K.: *The Gothic Revival*, London, Batsford, and New York, Holt Rinehart, 1963.

COLLINS, Peter: *Concrete: the Vision of a New Architecture*, London, Faber, and New York, Horizon, 1959.

COOPER, Douglas: *The Work of Graham Sutherland*, London, Lund, and New York, McKay, 1961.

DEAN, Beryl: *Ecclesiastical Embroidery*, London, Batsford, and Newton Centre, Mass., Brandford, 1958; *Church Needlework*, London, Batsford, and Newton Centre, Mass., Brandford, 1961.

HAMMOND, Peter: *Liturgy and Architecture*, London, Barry and Rockliff, and New York, Columbia Univ. Press, 1960.

LE CORBUSIER (JEANNERET, C. E. G.): *Towards a New Architecture*, New York, Praeger, 1959; *My Work*, London, Architectural Press, 1960.

MARITAIN, Jacques: *Art and Scholasticism*, New York, Scribners, 1962.

MUMFORD, Lewis: *Roots of Contemporary American Architecture*, New York, Grove Press, 1952.

OMAN, Charles: *English Church Plate, 597–1830*, London and New York, Oxford Univ. Press, 1957.

PORT, M. H.: *Six Hundred New Churches*, Naperville, Ill., Allenson, 1961.

RICHARDSON, E. P.: *Painting in America*, New York, Crowell, 1956.

RITCHIE, A. C.: *Sculpture of the Twentieth Century*, New York, Doubleday, 1953.

SMITH, G. E. K.: *New Architecture of Europe*, New York, Meridian, 1961.

SPENCE, Basil: *Phoenix at Coventry*, London, Faber, and New York, Harper, 1962.